Developing Supersensible Perception

"... a tour through the realms of consciousness that few could present. This book shows both detailed science and a refined humanities examination in service of painting the most precise and detailed picture of the deeper realms of reality."

JAMES D. RYAN, PH.D., PROFESSOR EMERITUS OF
ASIAN PHILOSOPHIES AND CULTURES AT THE
CALIFORNIA INSTITUTE OF INTEGRAL STUDIES

"What do you get when you mix degrees in electronics and mathematical engineering and a Ph.D. focused on philosophy, cosmology, and consciousness with Rudolf Steiner's theosophy, Patañjali's yoga, and psychedelic drugs? Hold on to your holographic hats, psychonauts, Shelli Joye will be your captain to the bubbling multiverse at the Planck length of space-time. Just be sure to bring your Fourier transform along so you can rematerialize in the explicate order when the trip is done."

TIMOTHY DESMOND, PH.D., AUTHOR OF
PSYCHE AND SINGULARITY

"This is not a book for the closed-minded! Shelli Joye's creative weaving of Steiner's insights—with threads drawn from yoga philosophy, quantum physics, electrical engineering, psychedelics, and alien encounters—is an invitation to walk, or dance, on the wild side of psychospiritual speculation."

SEAN KELLY, PH.D., AUTHOR OF *COMING HOME: THE BIRTH
AND TRANSFORMATION OF THE PLANETARY ERA*
AND *INDIVIDUATION AND THE ABSOLUTE*

"Shelli Joye takes the reader on a journey through the evolution of consciousness as described by Steiner, right to the frontier of sense-free thinking. She guides us with love, insight, and consummate intelligence into the heart of the mystery. An extraordinary book that achieves the seemingly impossible by articulating that which lies beyond the thinking mind."

". . . a wonderful synthesis of science and spirituality. The ideas in this book are challenging and elusive. The math is daunting. But it's burgeoning with understanding and insight. If you want to grapple with the "hard problem," here's a great place to start. And it might even help you develop a bit of perception beyond the ordinary. It's inspired me to pursue Rudolf Steiner's recommendations."

"Shelli Joye has done something important in bringing the early twentieth-century theosophy of Rudolf Steiner together with early twenty-first-century science. The reader will find in the first half of the book an insightful review of the theosophy of the past century illuminated both by the author's careful research and by her personal experience with the supersensible. In the second half, the author explains the challenging new neurophysics, which offers the scientific grounding that theosophy has up to now lacked. For readers not only in circles that are attuned to theosophy but also with those who sense a disassociation of doctrine and reality in their traditions."

"Joye's vivid, storied prose jaunts through the hinterlands of consciousness, offering a lucid interweaving of Steiner and Patañjali's technologies for navigating states of consciousness, traversing the subtle and manifest realms and their associated temporalities. Joye pays particular attention to physical and mathematical correlates of consciousness, including the role of the Fourier transform in translating between the temporal and atemporal—Bohm's explicate and implicate orders. Her keen intuition for seeing and explaining how things fit together reveals exactly the type of mind we need to lead us into the now burgeoning integral era."

Developing Supersensible Perception

Knowledge *of the* Higher Worlds through
Entheogens, Prayer, *and* Nondual Awareness

SHELLI RENÉE JOYE, Ph.D.

Inner Traditions
Rochester, Vermont

Inner Traditions
One Park Street
Rochester, Vermont 05767
www.InnerTraditions.com

Text stock is SFI certified

Cataloging-in-Publication Data for this title is available from the Library of Congress

ISBN 978-1-62055-875-1 (print)
ISBN 978-1-62055-876-8 (ebook)

Printed and bound in the United States by Lake Book Manufacturing, Inc.
The text stock is SFI certified. The Sustainable Forestry Initiative® program promotes sustainable forest management.

10 9 8 7 6 5 4 3 2 1

Text design and layout by Debbie Glogover
This book was typeset in Garamond Premier Pro with TT Supermolot Condensed and Gill Sans MT Pro used as display fonts

Chapters 7, 8, and the Appendix are based on the author's 2016 Ph.D. dissertation, "The Pribram-Bohm Holoflux Theory of Consciousness: An Integral Interpretation of the Theories of Karl Pribram, David Bohm, and Pierre Teilhard De Chardin," and also appeared in her books published by the Viola Institute in 2017: *Tuning the Mind: Geometries of Consciousness, The Little Book of Consciousness: Holonomic Brain Theory and the Implicate Order,* and *The Little Book of the Holy Trinity: A New Approach to Christianity, Indian Philosophy, and Quantum Physics.*

To send correspondence to the author of this book, mail a first-class letter to the author c/o Inner Traditions • Bear & Company, One Park Street, Rochester, VT 05767, and we will forward the communication.

*There slumber in every human being faculties by means
of which he can acquire for himself a knowledge of higher
worlds. . . . There remains only one question—how to set
to work to develop such faculties.*

RUDOLF STEINER,
KNOWLEDGE OF THE HIGHER WORLDS

Contents

The Scientific Basis of Extraordinary Experience

By Robert McDermott

This book is filled with philosophical reflections, scientific analyses, and spiritual practices; it is also an example of karma, the sometimes curvy line with a telos, an end in view. Shelli Joye's end, at least in this book, is a thoughtfully documented attempt to incorporate the works of Rudolf Steiner, Patañjali, Karl Pribram, and David Bohm in addressing what David Chalmers famously referred to in 1995 as "the hard problem of consciousness."

Let us first trace the lines of karma leading to this book. Were you to pass by a twelve-year-old in a library who is intently reading a book on hypnotism, you might not anticipate that, more than a half century later, this inquisitive preadolescent would publish a book that firmly links science, consciousness, and Rudolf Steiner's teachings on how to acquire supersensible perception.

Similarly, were you to follow the arc of this young student's academic career into her senior year of an engineering program, you might never predict that, after she had experienced an LSD-fueled night on a California beach and a mysterious encounter with what seemed to be a living ball of light by an ancient pool in the Texas hill country, this same student would be so deeply moved by these experiences that her professional interests would be shifted from engineering toward an intense lifelong study of Sanskrit, Patañjali's yoga, and Tantric meditation techniques.

What are the chances that this same young engineer, seeking to understand her experiences through books at the New York Public Library, would "just happen to notice," lying open on a table, a book called *In Search of the Miraculous* by the mathematician P. D. Ouspensky, and that this book would lead directly to the many works of Ouspensky, G. I. Gurdjieff, and eventually to Rudolf Steiner?

And what are the chances that this same young engineer, attending a workshop in New York, given by the mellifluent Taoist-Buddhist lecturer Alan Watts, would, upon hearing that he and other accomplished faculty had begun teaching Asian philosophies and religions at a new graduate school in San Francisco, leave her professional engineering job in the World Trade Center and move to San Francisco to study Sanskrit, esoteric philosophy, and meditation?

In her seventy years, Shelli Joye has sought to understand the miraculous, the transcendent, and the inner nature of things. She has practiced spiritual disciplines and sought deep insights. As is elaborated in this stunning book, she has gone even further, presenting a scientific basis for her extraordinary experiences.

When twenty-first-century individuals read a book by or about Steiner, or attend a lecture elaborating his ideas, they often seek more evidence to support his claims. This book offers such evidence. That she has titled her book *Developing Supersensible Perception* tells us that her life experience in many chapters makes a powerful claim that she has in fact accomplished what Steiner presented as natural for him and difficult, but certainly possible, for others.

Like Steiner, and many of those drawn on in this book to support esoteric principles with physics, Joye began her career in the hard sciences, first studying physics at Rice University and graduating with an electrical engineering degree. Steiner's own undergraduate degree from the Viennese Polytechnic Institute gave him a healthy respect for the scientific method, validated results, and affirmative evidence. He was certain that, in time, others would eventually validate his claims, even those claims that have until now been considered implausible by scientific criteria. This book represents a significant contribution toward providing a comprehensive scientific framework to support the worldview that Steiner and Joye hold in common and advance a century apart from each other.

One can only wonder what Steiner would make of Shelli Joye's enumeration of the five approaches to supersensible perception proposed in Patañjali's *Yoga Sūtra*: birth (karma), entheogens, prayer, psycho-spiritual exercises and practices (*tapas*), and contemplative meditation.

For many followers of Steiner, evidence for his esoteric claims to know higher worlds lies in two obviously successful applications of his ideas: the Waldorf approach to education and biodynamic agriculture. Following close behind is his work in anthroposophical medicine. All of these are evidential. Yet, until now, there have been very few efforts* to provide scientific evidence to validate Steiner. This book attempts to do just that.

The author first focuses primarily on Steiner and Patañjali, and the specific techniques they taught; she then presents her own experience and proceeds to build a supporting science of consciousness. Near the end, each chapter becomes more technical than its predecessor (e.g., with sections about "Spectral Flux and the Implicate Order" and "Holonomic Storage.") However, even readers not well versed in contemporary physics will find the author's exposition of Pribram, Bohm, and various scientific principles both understandable and encouraging. They reaffirm Steiner's case for supersensible knowledge as being valid and certainly worth the effort. One has to imagine that Steiner would be pleased, not just by Shelli's published words, but by the life experiences that made them possible.

ROBERT MCDERMOTT, PH.D., is president emeritus and a professor of philosophy and religion at the California Institute of Integral Studies (CIIS). He studied with the ecotheologian Thomas Berry and has published many essays, articles, and books, including *Steiner and Kindred Spirits* (2015) and *The New Essential Steiner: An Introduction to Rudolf Steiner for the 21st Century* (2009). McDermott is also the founding chair of the Sophia Project, an anthroposophic home in Oakland, California, for mothers and children at risk of homelessness.

---

*For an important, if slim, exception, see Arthur Zajonc, "Science and Anthroposophy," from the *Journal for Anthroposophy*, issue 81, 2010.

INTRODUCTION

Opening the Inner Eye
to New Dimensions

Our twenty-first century is popularly called the information age. Girding the planet, information technologies have literally wired the world into a weblike mesh of information links. Physically, all that can be seen of these links is metallic wire, fiber-optic cable, and orbiting satellites. But what do these physical links carry that is invisible to our ordinary senses? What might we see if we acquired supersensory vision?

If we had such vision, we would see human-encoded clouds of streaming electrons and photons buzzing through the wires and the cables, auroral clouds of glowing plasma swirling among and between our satellites through these wires, coursing along the physical links. From out of this vortex of radiance, our digital devices ceaselessly unpack and convert these vibrating energy spectra into the sounds, images, and text that we interact with, thereby allowing us to hear, see, and communicate with friends and strangers, far and near. Harnessed by our technical ingenuity, this radiant flux, this vast web of vibrating electromagnetic signals, emerges as the nervous system of our awakening global culture.

But many believe in (and have testified to) the existence of a vast range of *additional networks*, ancient webs of communication linking innumerable worlds and hidden dimensions far beyond those that our daily senses reveal. These rare *psychonauts** claim to have developed the ability to access new sensory modes of awareness. Their experiences

---

Psychonaut and *psychonautics*, from the Greek ψυχή, *psychē* ("soul," "spirit," or "mind") and ναύτης, *naútēs* ("sailor" or "navigator")—thus "sailor of the soul."

assure us that with sincere effort and sufficient practice, we too can soon awaken the latent ability within us, the ability to "see" for ourselves.

How I came to this knowledge is a story in itself. At the age of twelve, I discovered a book, *How to Hypnotize Your Friends,* describing the life and work of the Viennese physician Franz Anton Mesmer (1734–1815), known as the father of hypnotism and hypnotherapy.[1] According to the book, Mesmer's theory of "animal magnetism" is based on a mysterious, omnipresent, powerful living energy existing in nature. According to this theory, a living magnetic energy is continually flowing between and within all things. The book claimed that a diligent student could learn to sense, feel, and eventually to manipulate this magnetic energy, and thereafter one would be able to guide it as it flows through and beyond one's self, others, animals, and even crystals and rocks.* At the end of the book were listed a series of training exercises, suggestions to be cultivated and practiced until this animal magnetism could be sensed, developed, and controlled. Through regular practice, the book assured the reader, one would eventually master the technique required to hypnotize others through guidance and control of this animal magnetism.

The primary exercises, not at all difficult to do, were to be repeated daily, preferably at sunset or sunrise. One was to sit comfortably in a quiet, darkened room, lit only by at most a single candle flame, positioned at arm's length and close to eye level. Gazing steadily at the flame with eyelids half open, one should try to "let go of one's thoughts," or "empty one's mind," while making a sincere, sustained effort to drop any word, phrase, memory, or unbidden thought that would inevitably arise. The goal was to achieve complete "silence of mind," a challenge that intrigued my adolescent mind.

This contemplative practice early in my life did not last long, nor was I ever able to hypnotize my friends, but the concept and the practice did make a lasting impression on me, and one that resurfaced years later when, as a college student, I was thrown into what I could only

---

*This claim is reminiscent of both Chinese acupuncture and Japanese Reiki, as well as the traditional "laying on of hands" found in various cultures.

refer to as a gyrating galaxy of animal magnetism through the inges-tion of LSD-25 on a beach during summer vacation. Subsequently, I sought out whatever published material I could find on esoteric psy-chology, shamanism, and religious practices that I suspected were con-nected with consciousness transformation. I moved to New York City to find teachers, where masters of all persuasions could be found, from Tibetan *tulkus* to Zen masters. I worked in the World Trade Center by day, but spent my time in lectures, classes, and bookstores at night and on weekends, searching for clues on how to understand and operate consciousness. This eventually led to my "discovery" of Rudolf Steiner's book *An Occult Physiology* in a metaphysical bookstore in New York, and shortly after, the *Yoga Sūtra,* a handbook of contemplative practices by the fourth-century sage Patañjali, who lived in southern India. These two teachings took me far beyond my early encounter with Mesmer's work.

I was especially attracted to Steiner's work and the related fact that, during his lifetime, he traveled far beyond the conventional bounds of philosophy and engineering to explore consciousness through direct introspection; more importantly, Steiner was able to *convey* his expe-riences by contributing a vast record* of personal knowledge derived from this personal direct entry into supersensory networks. Steiner's published work offered in great detail a range of specific techniques (curiously, not unlike the book by Mesmer that had fascinated me in my youth), by which each one of us, with effort and practice, can activate supersensory-cognitive systems to both *perceive* these cosmic networks and *participate* in a myriad of vast dynamic networks of cosmic consciousness.

It is amusing to note that while Steiner's father, Johann, a telegraph operator for the Southern Austrian Railway, communicated with people invisible to him over a network of metallic wires with his telegraph key, his son, Rudolf, grew up to be a sort of *supersensible* telegraph operator,

---

*Rudolf Steiner produced over four hundred volumes of written material, which include his books and writings (about forty volumes) and over six thousand published transcriptions from his lectures.

communicating with invisible entities over invisible networks using his own "supersensory telegraph" mode of awareness.

The first four chapters of this book provide an expanded map of Rudolf Steiner's teachings upon which one can view his concepts as a consistent whole. In addition to practical techniques offered by Steiner, key instructions are also included from other sources, including from the fourth-century sage Patañjali. This material supports and extends Steiner's own approach to practice. Patañjali's *Yoga Sūtra* provides a clear account of techniques and stages leading to the state of nondual awareness, the state of *samādhi,** the experience of supersensible perception.

Chapter 5, "My Journey from Physics to Metaphysics," continues with a discussion of my experiences over several decades that led beyond a relatively exclusive focus on the physical sciences into more esoteric realms. Chapter 6 enumerates a wide range of Tantric approaches to supersensible perception from major schools of Indian yoga, and describes techniques from both northern and southern India. Among the important psychophysical concepts discussed are *mantra, yantra, chakra, samādhi,* and *kuṇḍalinī.* The final two chapters, "The Cosmology of Consciousness" and "The Physiology of Consciousness," offer a map of consciousness that supports and extends Steiner's approach to understanding consciousness, a map that is based directly on the work of the brain scientist Karl Pribram (1919–2015) and theoretical physicist David Bohm (1917–1992). The book concludes with a description of the physiology of consciousness within the human body and suggestions for further research.

I have provided an appendix, "The Mathematics of Consciousness," offering a step-by-step derivation of Euler's formula of 1784. This famous equation indicates how space-time directly links to a mysterious transcendental dimension. This relationship, the basis of the Fourier transform, underlies all of our twenty-first-century electronics and networks and establishes the ontological basis for supersensible perception.

Samādhi is best translated as a state of nondual awareness in which the universe is suddenly sensed to be completely interconnected, but the term is often translated as "meditation."

One result of practicing Steiner's exercises is a change in one's dreams; from being vague and distorted, they take on a more orderly pattern. A further change is a kind of continuity of consciousness; one's ego awareness is strengthened in sleep and is retained during dreams, much like the phenomena of "lucid dreaming." Another result is a perception of the aura, the astral form that envelops our physical body; likewise the refinement of the chakras, those centers of esoteric force which theosophy claims existed within the physical body.

GARY LACHMAN,
RUDOLF STEINER: AN INTRODUCTION TO HIS LIFE AND WORK (2007), 138–39.

1

Five Approaches to Supersensible Perception

STEINER'S SUPERSENSIBLE PERCEPTION

In 1904, Rudolf Steiner began his *Knowledge of the Higher Worlds and Its Attainment* with a sentence that well encapsulates the basic premise of his entire perception and teaching.

> There slumber in every human being faculties by means of which he can acquire for himself a knowledge of higher worlds.... There remains only one question—how to set to work to develop such faculties.[1]

Steiner himself worked diligently throughout most of his adult life to develop and improve his own ability to use these new sensory modes of direct perception that lay distinctly beyond touch, smell, hearing, or sight. In his writings and lectures, he refers to this new development among sensory capabilities as "supersensible perception." He describes with great enthusiasm how, through use of this new sense, he has been able to explore and navigate a dimension that is generally far beyond everyday human awareness.

He tells us that, above all, the greatest value he has discovered through his exploration of the supersensible lies in the direct knowledge and guidance he receives through interacting not only with the hierarchies of beings he discovers in these dimensions (which he refers to as angels), but through the direct connection he is able to establish with what he calls the Akashic records, a vast repository of information, a dynamic record of all events, thoughts, words, and feelings ever to have occurred in the past or to be currently emerging.

Steiner insists that it is of the greatest importance for human society that each individual makes the effort to open one's inner eye to these hidden realities by consistent effort, following specific exercises and approaches that will ultimately establish healthy new channels of direct communication with our ancestors, our planet, and a wide range of transcendent entities (angels of various hierarchies). In his many lectures and books, we find the clear description of methods and means by which a human being can begin to nourish, activate, and operate this latent ability of supersensory perception.

According to Steiner, this potential for supersensory perception is found in every human being at various stages of development, and he goes on to say that when the internal organs of supersensory perception have evolved to the point at which they begin to open to this new awareness, one experiences it as an awakening to a "higher self."

> In addition to what we may call the ordinary, everyday self, everyone also bears a higher self, a higher human being, within. This higher human being remains hidden until awakened. It can be awakened only as each individual awakens it inwardly. Until then, those latent higher faculties within each of us, which lead to supersensory knowledge, remain hidden.[2]

Steiner himself was the product of a nineteenth-century Viennese academic social milieu, and his lectures and writings were directed at such an audience. The modern reader may grasp Steiner's concepts more clearly by considering alternate paradigms, one ancient and one from the twenty-first century. Accordingly, in examining Steiner's description of the means to acquiring supersensory perception, we will find clear parallels in Indian philosophy (specifically the *Yoga Sūtra* of Patañjali), and also consider how these parallels appear to be directly supported by recent cutting-edge concepts published in the field of quantum biology and quantum brain dynamics (QBD).[3]

SUPERSENSIBLE KNOWLEDGE:
HOW TO OBTAIN IT

Steiner insists that throughout history and within all cultures there have been those who, using various methods and techniques, have learned to activate newly evolving organs of supersensible perception. Subsequently, these rare individuals experienced direct contact with an entire world heretofore invisible to them.

> Mystics, Gnostics, Theosophists—all speak of a world of soul and spirit which for them is just as real as the world which we see with our physical eyes and touch with our physical hands.[4]

Steiner points out the dangers of *not* developing the power of supersensory cognition. He cautions that without the ability to perceive the rich hierarchy of entities by which we are surrounded,* modern humans have become, like blind deer in a forest, vulnerable prey to a host of unperceived entities, causing enormous personal grief, social unrest, and even disease. Without the full evolutionary emergence of supersensible perceptual knowledge, the modern human is at the whim of many of these supersensible forces, for both good and bad. However, once equipped with the ability to perceive these entities, much suffering can be avoided, and crucial knowledge for dealing with the problems of the world can be obtained. But how does the individual initially acquire sufficient clear knowledge to activate this supersensible perception, and where does one begin to look for such knowledge in our modern disenchanted world?

According to Steiner, although a rare few may have been born with supersensible perception, attaining it is a lifetime project for most people, who must learn for themselves how to develop these faculties. Classically, there are five possibilities for obtaining this knowledge.

---

*Various cultures have called them angels, demons, celestial beings, spirits, *devas*, and so on.

It is Steiner's conviction that humanity is now ready for a widespread acquisition of supersensible perception, whereas in centuries past, the blossoming of this new sense was limited to a rare handful of mystics, philosophers, and gnostics, from whose writings and handed-down teachings we still might learn. In fact, the process required to develop higher faculties of perception has been well documented as far back as the fourth century CE, where we find in Patañjali's *Yoga Sūtra* (IV.1) a description of five primary ways in which an individual finds his or her way to these powers of supersensible perception (in Sanskrit called *siddhis*, i.e., "powers," "attainments," "accomplishments"). Here is the opening line of the fourth and final chapter of Patañjali's *Yoga Sūtra:*

Sūtra IV.1

Janmauṣadhi-mantra-tapaḥ-samādhi-jāḥ siddhayaḥ[5]
*The supersensory powers of perception arise from birth,
drugs, prayer, psychophysical exercises, meditation*

The general pattern of this type of teaching mnemonic, called in Sanskrit a *śloka* (*shloka*), or verse line, is that the order of presentation is of great significance. Words introduced first in the śloka are given greater emphasis in the teaching, carrying more weight in the topic or statement being made. The sequence is also indicative of an order or evolution in time. In this important śloka that opens the final chapter in the *Yoga Sūtra*, the five ways of acquiring siddhis ("supersensible perception") are, in order of efficacy, as follows:

1. By Birth (*janma*, genetic disposition)
2. By Drugs (*oṣadhi*, entheogens)
3. By Prayer (*mantra*, silent or audible verbal repetition)
4. By Psychophysical Exercises (*tapas*, self-discipline, exercises)
5. By Meditation (*samādhi*, trance)

ACQUISITION BY BIRTH
Genetic Disposition

In his *Yoga Sūtra*, Patañjali mentions acquisition by birth as a first and primary attribute for initial success in seeking to awaken the organs of supersensible perception. At birth, each newborn human possesses innumerable traits, characteristics, and potentials inherited from a broad and diverse stream of personalities through the unique genetic material contributed by father and mother. These genetic data recordings have been forged and accumulated during millennia of ancestral experience. The inherited traces remain superpositioned within the physical genome as information that is available as needed for the survival, growth, and development of the individual human being.

Rudolf Steiner was likely among the relatively small number of human beings to have been born with the genetic disposition optimized for early blossoming of the power of supersensory perception. However, for those without such specific genetic advantages at birth, there are the additional four approaches (drugs, prayer, exercise, meditation) listed by Patañjali in *Yoga Sūtra* IV.1.

ACQUISITION BY DRUGS
Entheogens

In 1885, the first annotated translation of Patañjali's *Yoga Sūtra* was published by Tatya Tookeram, a fellow of the Theosophical Society.[6] Steiner himself had first become interested in the Theosophical Society as a first-year student in Vienna, and by 1885, the twenty-four-year-old enthusiastically attended most lectures and conferences offered by the Society. It is quite likely that he was familiar with this early translation of the *Yoga Sūtra*, which was widely circulated within the Society that year. In the commentary on *sūtra* IV.1, we find the following:

> The *siddhis* or "perfections" [supersensible perception] produced by herbs consist of elixirs and the like, that is, supernatural herbs; this

perfection is obtained by persons who possess knowledge of these supernatural herbs or medicines.[7]

According to Patañjali, many seekers discover that their initial experience of supersensory perception is attained most readily by ingestion of drugs (called *oṣadhi* in the Sanskrit of the *Yoga Sūtra*). Many of these traditional entheogens, perception-changing organic compounds created within certain plants and mushrooms, were discovered and widely used in the ancient world. The preparation and use of a psychedelic drink called *soma* is well documented in the *Rig Veda*, which is thought to have been composed in northern India over 3,500 years ago. In the *Rig Veda* (8.48.3) we find the following line:

> *We have drunk soma and become immortal;*
> *we have attained the light, the Gods discovered.*[8]

Within such plants can be found amazingly complex hydrocarbon molecules that slowly break down and dissolve in the warmth of a coursing ionic bloodstream. As they decompose, the molecular structures release their unique electromagnetic "signature" spectrums. This radiant energy within the bloodstream immediately interacts with and resonates within the electromagnetic plasma throughout the entire blood-capillary system, driving normal human consciousness into new regions of experience.

It seems reasonable to wonder whether Steiner himself may have experimented with such substances in his search for entry into other dimensions of perception. Many plant-derived drugs that are illegal now were perfectly legal during Steiner's lifetime. From approximately 1880 to 1920, for example, the Viennese medical community documented the acceptable use of cannabis, opium, hashish, laudanum, cocaine, and other mind-altering substances derived from plant material. In modern terms such drugs are known as *entheogens* or *psychedelics*.

The early mind-expanding use of such substances as soma (currently thought to be psychedelic mushrooms or cannabis) has been described in ancient Vedic hymns (circa 2400 BCE). In addition to this, a hallucinatory rye-ergot compound is known to have been used by the ancient Greeks in Delphic oracle ceremonies. Explorers of the psyche have discovered a wide range of these compounds that are classified as *entheogens*—psychotropic substances used for spiritual development. Early Buddhist monks in China, for example, discovered a warm drink made from an infusion of tea leaves to be highly conducive to long hours of meditative contemplation. Contemporary psychonauts often use *Cannabis sativa* and caffeine (tea or coffee) as aids during contemplative sessions to more quickly reach states of supersensible perception.

Organic oṣadhi found in nature include *Psilocybe cubensis* mushrooms, ayahuasca vine, cannabis, peyote, and *Salvia divinorum*, among many others. With the advent of modern chemistry an even wider range of new manufactured psychotropics have been synthesized. These so-called "designer drugs" of the twentieth and twenty-first century include LSD-25, DMT, MDMA, and countless other synthetic oṣadhi.

In the nineteenth century, Vienna was known as "the mecca of medicine," and medical compounds and formulations flowed in to the medical community from all parts of the vast Hapsburg Empire. As early as 1855, a Viennese physician, Ernst Freiherr von Bibra (1806–1878), published a book that discussed the clinical usage of hashish for over thirty pages. In addition to his recorded description of numerous beneficial outcomes in his treatment of patients with the strong mind-altering effects of hashish, von Bibra describes his own self-experiments with hashish. His conclusion was as follows:

> Recent experiments and experiences made on the medical effect of the hemp plant and its compounds very much point to their advantage and are highly recommended.[9]

Other publications in the late nineteenth century supported the widespread positive experiences in the medicinal applications of cannabis.

> Typically, doctors who worked intensively with cannabis drugs for years would classify them as valuable medicines.[10]

In addition to cannabis, an even stronger entheogen was widely available. Cocaine, which had first been distilled in Vienna in 1855 through the processing of coca leaves, was widely reputed to work as a miracle drug and proved to be capable of curing alcoholism and morphine addiction. It is well known that Sigmund Freud (1856–1939), who was only five years older than Steiner, began experimenting with cocaine about the same time that Steiner was an engineering student in Vienna. Records still exist of a delivery in April 1884 from Angel's Pharmacy in Vienna to Sigmund Freud, who was twenty-eight at the time.[11]

In 1879, Steiner's family had relocated to the small town of Inzersdorf, five miles south of Vienna, where, encouraged by his father, Rudolf had applied to and then been accepted into an engineering program at the Vienna Institute of Technology. During the next two years, his primary subjects of study were mathematics, physics, and chemistry. However, he continued to be intrigued by metaphysical ideas of an otherworldly nature and was strongly attracted to the emerging ideas of theosophy and the occult, then at the height of fashion among university students in Vienna. To attend classes, Steiner rode the commuter train between his home and the Institute in Vienna, and before long he grew to recognize and greet many fellow travelers who habitually shared the same cabin. Among the most interesting of his newfound acquaintances was an elderly herb gatherer named Felix Kogutzki.

Many years later, Steiner wrote that the relatively uneducated Kogutzki was an authentic expert on the habitat and specific usage of plants and herbs that grew in profusion in the thick forests of the Vienna Woods, a vast unoccupied range of hills and valleys forested with oaks, beeches, and tall black firs southwest of Vienna. He wrote in his biography that Kogutzki was "completely initiated into the secrets of the plants and their effects, and into their connection with the cosmos and human nature."[12]

Clearly, Steiner was impressed with Kogutzki and wanted to learn everything he could from the herbalist. On weekends, he was soon visiting Kogutzki's cabin in Trumau, a village considerably farther from

Vienna than was Steiner's home station. It is easy to imagine that in Kogutzki's cabin, or during their overnight excursions in the Vienna Woods, Steiner may indeed have experimented with various entheogenic herbal substances introduced under the guidance of Kogutzki.

According to Steiner, Kogutzki had developed his own deeply spiritual knowledge directly from nature and herbs, and stated that with Kogutzki, "It was possible to speak with someone of the spiritual world as with someone of deep experience."[13] In fact, as Steiner relates in his biography, it was Kogutzki who first introduced him to the person or the entity whom Steiner later referred to as "the Master," an important development in Steiner's growing capacity for supersensible perception of other worlds.

ACQUISITION BY PRAYER
Chanting, Silent or Audible Prayer Repetition

Patañjali includes *mantra* third in his list of major factors useful in the initial quest to acquire supersensible perception. The Sanskrit word *mantra* is itself a combination of the word *man,* "the thinking mind" and *tra,* "crossing" or "traversing." These mantras, repetitions of short rhythmical phrases, have been found by sages throughout the ages to be extremely effective as tools with which to bridge the mental activity of the brain, allowing awareness to pass beyond discursive thought into what Steiner terms the Silence. This process entails a shift of focus, a relocating of one's center of gravity of awareness inwardly, below the verbal-level activity, into the nonverbal (preverbal) regions of consciousness. A scholarly definition of mantra can be found in volume 4 of the *History of Ancient Indian Religion* (1975).

> A mantra may, etymologically speaking and judging from the usage prevailing in the oldest texts, approximately be defined as follows: word(s) believed to be of "superhuman origin," received, fashioned and spoken by the "inspired" seers, poets and reciters in order to evoke divine power(s) and especially conceived as means of creating,

conveying, concentrating and realizing intentional and efficient thought, and of coming into touch or identifying oneself with the essence of the divinity which is present in the mantra.[14]

This description of mantra indicates how this practice may be easily understood by other traditions as a type of prayer. In Eastern Christianity, the widespread use of the Jesus Prayer, practiced by monks and hermits for centuries, falls under this definition, as does the Rosary (a series of Our Fathers and Hail Marys) recited by Roman Catholics, or the Takbir, Allahu Akbar ("God is Great"), frequently recited by Muslims. The Hindu use of the mantra *Om* is widely known, as is the famous Tibetan mantra, *Oṃ maṇi padme hūṃ*.

The practical importance of such mantric prayer repetition as a practical aid for developing supersensible perception cannot be underestimated. The habitual operations of the mind present a discursive flow of ideas. Any pause in the stream of thought is quickly filled with previously subliminal thoughts, ideas, and memories that are always waiting to emerge from just below the threshold of awareness. It has been said that "nature abhors a vacuum" (a comment credited to Aristotle), and a common human experience is that the moment the mind finds itself without an object of focus, new thoughts and memories flood into awareness. Repetition of a short mantric prayer helps to counter this habitual reaction by giving the mind something to work with, allowing the deeper observer to detach and move away from everyday mental activity. The basic mechanisms of the mind are kept marginally occupied while the contemplative's awareness is allowed to move toward a more complete silence devoid of the distraction of discursive ideas, thoughts, and memories.

On a more esoteric level, the words and intentions of the mantra or prayer, through repetition, plant whatever idea, image, or injunction that may be associated with the phrase ever more deeply within the subconscious of the practitioner. Like water following the same channel, the imprinted influence grows ever deeper. With sufficient repetition, deep resonances build up in the vast web of reality that is everywhere connected. This psychophysical science of mantric prayer is discussed at greater length in chapter 6, "Indian Tantra and Supersensible Perception."

ACQUISITION BY PSYCHOPHYSICAL EXERCISES
Self-Discipline, Austerities, Mental Focus, Development of Will

The fourth way mentioned, *tapas*, includes self-imposed exercises designed to develop the will and focus the consciousness, practicing austerities such as fasting, physical activities and sports, hatha yoga, and *prāṇāyāma* (its modern equivalent being holotropic breathwork). Unfortunately, the term *yoga* itself is almost exclusively seen by modern Western society as being hatha yoga, although the *Yoga Sūtra* goes far beyond the hatha yoga poses, or *āsanas*. Apparently, few Western hatha yoga teachers have carefully studied the *Yoga Sūtra*, or they would have easily discovered that hatha yoga is simply one of the eight major approaches to an integration of mind, body, and spirit encouraged by Patañjali.

Tapas includes a wide range of psychophysical exercises and practices. While hatha yoga is primarily a focus on integrating the physical body through various poses and stretches, the more significant purposes for practicing these poses include the development of willpower and the ability to focus consciousness on specific locations within the body, and then to maintain this focus of awareness for an extended time period. The practice generates internal heat or energy, and in fact the Sanskrit root of *tapas* is identical to the word *heat*. Other tapas, exercises that require willpower, effort, and regular practice, include cultivating the qualities of gentleness, sincerity, honesty, humility, faith, and perhaps, above all, patience.

ACQUISITION BY MEDITATION
Contemplation, Silent Awareness, Trance

The Sanskrit word *samādhi* best encapsulates Steiner's approach to non-dual awareness, and the term is described and developed at length in the

Yoga Sūtra. Attaining to the state of samādhi may be considered the primary method for developing supersensible perception as described in Steiner's writings and lectures.

There are many translations of the *Yoga Sūtra* in which Patañjali's details regarding the technique of samādhi are made the primary focus of discussion. This method, mentioned last by Patañjali in *Yoga Sūtra* IV.1, is recommended in a subsequent sūtra as the most reliable, repeatable, and direct technique for development of the faculty of supersensible perception, and knowledge of samādhi is required for entrance into these wider realms of being.

It is likely that Steiner first encountered this powerful technique during his early twenties as he grew more involved with the Theosophical Society, founded in 1875 by H. P. Blavatsky when the inquisitive young Steiner himself was only fourteen. As noted above, in 1885, the first translation of Patañjali's *Yoga Sūtra,* which Steiner himself may have read, was published by the Theosophical Society.[15] It is interesting to find the emphasis on "supernatural herbs or medicines" (previously quoted) in Tookeram's translation and commentary on the sūtra we have been studying, IV.1.

Steiner became deeply involved in the Theosophical Society during his years in Vienna and grew increasingly active at organizational meetings and public events. He was so instrumental in its growth that he eventually was appointed general secretary of the German Theosophical Society. Even with this deep involvement, however, he was not completely happy with the Society's focus on things that he considered spurious and nonscientific. He was in particular disagreement with efforts to regard a young Indian man, Jiddu Krishnamurti, as the new spiritual world teacher of the era, much in the same way that Jesus Christ had been regarded in the first century CE. Eventually, Steiner broke with the Theosophists and established his own organization in 1912, calling his the Anthroposophical Society.*

---

*From an amalgam of Greek terms: *anthropos* = "human," and *sophia* = "wisdom."

MOTIVATION IN A DISENCHANTED UNIVERSE

Unfortunately, modern technology has made the chances of widespread development of supersensible organs of perception even less likely by disenchanting the universe, fostering a tendency of dismissal toward any possibility of contacting an invisible world unrecognized by science. Indeed, the popular view is that *only* what can be seen and touched by normal human waking senses is real, while the current scientific view insists that *only* what is proven and verified through repeatable, physical scientific testing is real.*

Protectors of the modern paradigm of science hold that *even to consider* the possible existence of other dimensions or entities existing (configurations or beings that somehow might be perceivable if we had the right sense organs) is folly and a waste of time. Furthermore, they contend that as topics for research these activities are judged to be a complete waste of money and resources better spent on "real" observations obtained through experiments in space and time.

Countering this general trend, Steiner challenges us to overcome our culturally disenchanted prejudices by rising up to actively seek knowledge of the supersensible. He urges each individual to find a way to accumulate a wide range of what he calls "initiation-knowledge," sufficient to kindle the required motivation to begin actual practice. It is only through individual, personal effort to seek out, discover, and put into regular practice concrete methods and techniques that one can rise to the next stage in cognitive evolution and begin at last to access the wider supersensible cosmos.

Along with such a personal, immediate perception of the supersensible cosmos, there will dawn a deeper self-knowledge gained through supersensible perception, a supersensible self-knowledge. This then becomes the driving force in Steiner's writings and lectures. As Steiner described in a lecture in Wales on August 19, 1923, "Genuine

---

*In this regard, it can be seen as highly ironic that millions depend on truly invisible dimensions to carry their cell phone conversations, texting, tweeting, and internet images daily—for who has seen, felt, tasted, or touched an electromagnetic radio wave?

self-knowledge must be sought to-day through inner development, by calling up forces in the soul not previously there."[16]

CREATION OF SUPERSENSIBLE SENSE ORGANS

But in seeking supersensible self-knowledge, how might a modern human being living through a normally socialized ego give birth to this new, higher (or deeper) being within us? Steiner says that at the very beginning one must make a great and sincere effort to perceive that which is beyond space and the normal sensory realm.

> He must summon up from within himself cognitional powers which are not bound up with his senses or his perception of space.[17]

Access to this higher knowledge requires first the development of, and then the ability to control and use, the supersensible sense organs.

Steiner says that meditation is the first primary tool that should be studied, practiced, and mastered on the path to developing these organs of supersensible perception. In his book *Knowledge of the Higher Worlds and Its Attainment*, Steiner tells us:

> The life of the soul in thought, which gradually widens into a life in spiritual being, is called by Gnosis and by Spiritual Science, *Meditation* (contemplative reflection). This meditation is the means to supersensible knowledge.[18]

It may be said that one of Steiner's primary goals in his teaching is to convince contemporary human beings that there *is* another reality in which we live, a higher ego to be experienced, a radical extension beyond what we normally take to be thought and perception. But he insists that, for most people, this new mode or function can only be entered into consciously if we first develop the requisite new "supersensory sense organs" through practice of the techniques called meditation. In fact, through learning to meditatively focus supersensible energy currents into the newly manifesting supersensory sense organs, the contemplative soon begins to experience a new mode of awareness that grows in clarity as the organs gain strength.

> Such supersensible currents in the human organism always express themselves by creating for themselves also a physical sense-organ.[19]

And how soon can one expect results when beginning to develop these supersensible organs of perception? Steiner simply answers, "It is of no importance how far anyone can go in a given time; the point is that he should earnestly seek."[20]

2

Activating and Cultivating
Supersensible Perception

While a rare few humans, like Steiner, are born with supersensory organs fully developed and functioning, most of us must apply other steps in order to cultivate, activate, and directly "see" using these newly emergent faculties for perception within supersensory dimensional webs. The first step is to understand what may be an astonishing idea to many: that there are indeed other ways of thinking, other ways of operating our conscious mind stuff. The first step toward development of supersensible perception is to accept the possibility (which was, to Steiner, the reality) that there are indeed other operational modes of our conscious mind, accessible only if we know how to activate them. Steiner tells us that in the early stages of developing non-ordinary modes of awareness, in addition to practicing meditation, we should focus on activating and strengthening the *three categories of thinking*: imaginative thinking, active thinking, and intuitive thinking.

THE THREE CATEGORIES OF THINKING

Imaginative Thinking

Imaginative thinking is the dominant mode of our modern age, and Steiner believes it is actually a form of passive thinking. It is passive because it depends on sensory information from the external world being fed passively into our receptive cognitive systems, where it is then, at some future time—whether days or microseconds—recalled from the past, taken out of mental storage, processed, and re-created as an image, or a

21

series of images. Results and conclusions drawn by imaginative thinking are sent back to memory and preserved there, for a time, either long-term or short-term, in our human memory storage bank. Imaginative thinking requires *holographic images* retrieved from memory.

Our schools have taught us to approach thinking in this way. When we want to "think," we actually enter into what Steiner calls imaginative thinking. We set in motion this pattern in our system of thought that retrieves previously stored memory data and compares the information thus retrieved with other called-up memory data. Of course, our mental thinking in this mode can perform logic and perceive the operations of such logic being performed on our called-up memories, mostly abstracted and restrained through the use of the symbolic system we call words, manipulated with the syntax of what we call language.

Developed from an early age, this mode of thinking is typically the only way of thinking taught to and learned by contemporary students. Modern technology only reinforces imaginative thinking among humans by making the written word and the visual images pervasive and ubiquitous at every turn, through media such as handheld digital devices, laptop computers, billboards, radio, and television. These ensure that human beings are constantly occupied with the abstraction of word, language, and memory, or, to use a common phrase, "To think is to speak."

Humans have seemingly lost the will and ability to suspend imaginative thinking, to stop the internal verbal flow, which, like the sorcerer's apprentice,* once begun, never seems to stop. They have no idea how to entertain the pregnant silence so requisite for other modes of communication, higher modes of thinking.

But Steiner discovered and explored new and more sophisticated modes of thinking, ways of using the mind to grasp regions of aware-

---

The Sorcerer's Apprentice (German: *Der Zauberlehrling*) is a poem by Goethe, written in 1797. The poem begins as an old sorcerer departs his workshop, leaving his apprentice with chores to perform. Tired of fetching water by pail, the apprentice enchants a broom to do the work for him—using magic in which he is not yet fully trained. The floor is soon awash with water, and the apprentice realizes that he cannot stop the broom because he has never learned the command "to cease."

ness previously unimaginable. Both Steiner and Patañjali discovered that the conventional operating systems of the human mind and brain can definitely be reprogrammed to offer new capabilities, much as contemporary computer devices can be upgraded. Similar ideas for actively evolving human thinking capacities are discussed by the American neuroscientist John Lilly in his 1968 book, *Programming and Metaprogramming in the Human Biocomputer: Theory and Experiments*. Nevertheless, the majority of modern human individuals continue, for the most part, to operate within a conventional and somewhat restrictive linear mode of thought. Due to over-reliance on previously learned words, images, and concepts, such linear thinking unknowingly operates within the verbal straitjacket of convention that Steiner calls *imaginative thinking*. Being so constrained, imaginative thinkers assume that theirs is the only possible mode of thought. Steiner, however, speaking from personal knowledge, works to help others break out of the limiting trap of imaginative thinking by describing an entirely new mode of using the mind. He calls this improved mode *active thinking*.

Active Thinking

What Steiner calls active thinking is neither passive in the way he has described imaginative thinking, nor is it found to be operational in most humans. By contrast, active thinking is a mode of powerful cognition that can be cultivated and developed through the efforts of the individual. Though seldom taught, it is a powerful tool that, used in conjunction with meditation, hastens the awakening of supersensible cognition.

> For the first step in those methods for developing inner forces of the soul leading to supersensible cognition, called by us meditation and concentration, is by finding the way over from purely passive thinking to thinking that is inwardly active.[1]

As previously described, ordinary thinking is passive; it does not reach out and touch anything, it simply "presents itself to be hit."[2] By contrast, active thinking requires an intention of will, a direction, and a certain sense of feeling or touch. In fact, Steiner says, this "is a first step, but we must take this step, this turning of one's own thinking into active thinking, into an organ of touch."[3] He goes on to conclude that discovery of and exercise of active thinking will lead eventually to contact with or to a *touching* of the spiritual world itself.

> We reach the stage of living spiritually in the world in such a way that thinking develops into a touching . . . we learn to touch in the spiritual world, to make contact with it, to enter into a living relation with it.[4]

What does Steiner mean here by *touching* as it relates to thinking? To Steiner, this thinking mode that involves touching is a sort of cognitive sensing without words, a truly tactile willed experience, the contact of mental stuff with something in some locus of space, time, and perhaps reaching into other dimensions. And it is active thinking that leads to and opens up for us the possibilities for what Steiner calls intuitive thinking.

Intuitive Thinking

Intuitive thinking is a special form of cognition higher than our ordinary mental activity and a step beyond active thinking. It is required for communication with and knowledge of the true Self. Steiner classifies this special form of cognition with the word *intuition*. We should not be confused, he says, with the general use of the term *intuition* by which is denoted certain sensitive or dim feelings, which themselves are "a kind of shadow picture."[5] On the contrary, Steiner says, "True Intuition is itself the highest form of cognition possible for man on Earth."[6]

In fact the word *intuition* stems from the Latin word *intueri*, which can be translated as "to look inside" or "to contemplate."[7] The French philosopher Henri Bergson (1859–1941), who won the Nobel Prize in Literature in 1927 and was a contemporary of Steiner, wrote and lectured extensively on the importance of intuition as a means of obtaining knowledge. Bergson believed, as did Steiner, that intuition is a faculty of consciousness that can take us into deeper understanding than the intellect.

When Steiner describes this intuitive thinking as the method for "developing inner forces of the soul leading to supersensible cognition . . . called by us meditation and concentration,"[8] we are reminded of the well-known opening injunction from that fourth-century CE classic of contemplative meditation, Patañjali's *Yoga Sūtra*:

Sūtra I.2

Yogaś-citta-vṛtti-nirodhaḥ

Yoga is the silencing of the activity of the brain-mind.[9]

This quiet contemplation or meditation leads to the stillness requisite for the manifestation of what Steiner terms intuitive thinking. Initially, our mind continues "to think" on its own momentum, in its own relatively limited, verbally cognitive habituated manner. We lack the understanding that there may be other ways "to think" without the constraining requirement of word manipulation and memory retrieval.

But in the beginning, attaining to supersensible perception requires the stilling of *at least* three activities: (1) the mind's external sensory processing activity, (2) the gratuitous formation of strings of cognitive verbal code (words), and (3) the storing and retrieving of memories. We find further corroboration from Saint Isaac the Syrian, a contemplative who lived in what is now eastern Saudi Arabia in the seventh century CE.

> When the senses, however, are confined by stillness and not permitted to venture forth, and by its aid the soul's memories grow old, then you will see what are the soul's natural thoughts, what is the nature of the soul, and what treasures she has hidden within herself. These treasures are the perception of things incorporeal.[10]

Intuitive thinking then is not verbal thinking; it is not the internal silent articulation of human language, of words threaded together in a sequential time stream, but categorically a qualitatively different kind of thinking. Intuitive thinking, contemplation, or to Patañjali, samādhi, is a more direct, richer category of "thinking" that is, if anything, ninety degrees to the normal time stream of thinking, reminding us of the similar contrast in computer technology between linear computing and parallel computing. Intuitive thinking offers the simplicity of direct communication, communion, or resonance between the ordinary ego and the true "I" existing in a supersensible world.

But first attempts at even beginning to move toward such a state of silence and simplicity are often frustrated by seemingly sticky attachment to rising memories and unreserved attention to, and focus on, new thoughts. We discover, to our surprise, that much of our ordinary verbal thinking and attention processes seem to be a series of habitual sequences of cognitive patterns, programmed and reinforced by countless repetitions, and now seemingly beyond our conscious control. Steiner reassures us, however, that if we patiently persevere, we will eventually begin to discover this new "silence of inner thinking" and find it, to our surprise, to be more real, more significant, more satisfying than the external sensory world, from which we have learned to think only with the obfuscating tools of language abstraction.[11]

The critical questions for Steiner are these: How do we go about learning the requisite stilling of what at first seems to be these unrelenting changing states of the mind, like waves on a beach? How and where do we learn the techniques that would allow us to move beyond our habitual way of thinking? How do we reprogram our consciously cognitive processes? How do we meditate? Steiner answers:

> The first step in those methods for developing inner forces of the soul leading to supersensible cognition, called by us meditation and concentration, is by finding the way over from purely passive thinking to thinking that is inwardly active.[12]

But where do we learn how to take these first steps toward this new way of thinking that leads to supersensible cognition?

THREE WAYS OF LEARNING

Steiner says, "The knowledge leading over from the world of the senses to the supersensible has been called, throughout the ages, initiation-knowledge."[13] But there are three ways of acquiring initiation-knowledge, and he describes these three avenues to learning supersensible cognition.

Learning through Inner Activity

In his first answer, perhaps more of a warning, he says that we must focus on something that does not deal with memory, for "in memory all manner of vague impressions cling to our concepts."[14] Furthermore, if we focus on a concept, it should correspond to a reality, yet be something active. It could be a single concept, like a Japanese Zen koan, or a short prayer, or mantra, or even an internal visualization of various loci within the physical body. But how do we initially discover what works for us? Steiner says that there are three possibilities. The first and perhaps simplest step is for us to create our own object of meditation, to develop and practice our own method of inner prayer "through our own inner activity."[15]

Learning through a Teacher

Another possibility is the "guru" route. Steiner says that "the second way is to go to someone with experience." However, the danger is that one might become emotionally dependent on this teacher, as often happens. Steiner stresses again that every action, every step on the path must be taken independently and with courage through one's own inner activity. At all costs, he says, avoid dependency on another.[16] Each person must find his or her own unique way, discoverable through trial and error. Depending too heavily on the exhortation and examples of another, no matter how wise or evolved the individual may be, might cause us to miss the very thing that is most appropriate, and even necessary, for our own unique current situation and stage of growth. Developing the skill of freely trusting our own choices and acting on them increases the possibility of being able to *intuit* what we most need in every situation.

Learning through an Image or Book

And for those who cannot find or perhaps do not want to follow a living guru, and yet do not have the confidence to develop their own inner practice or techniques of meditation, there is yet another way to acquire what is needed for progress.

> And finally, the third way. Instruction can be sought from a teacher who—one might say—remains invisible. The student takes a book he has never seen before, opens it at random and reads any chance sentence. He can thus be sure of coming on something entirely new to him, and then he must work on it with inner activity. A subject for meditation can be made of the sentence, or perhaps of some illustration or diagram in the book.[17]

Here we receive teaching intuitively, visually, and via the written word. To Steiner, this seems to be better than the second approach, that of finding a living teacher or guru. This "way of the book" avoids the risk of falling into a complicated sticky web of relationships with a human teacher, a relationship that can all too quickly grow into infatuation, submission, and projection. Steiner repeatedly urges absolute freedom for the seeker, a freedom that leads to the self-confidence born of sustained effort, but definitely requiring the full emotional freedom of choice.

> People who begin to have some presentiment of supersensible things are apt to wax talkative on the subject, thereby retarding their normal development. The less one talks about these matters the better.[18]

Steiner's warning here indicates an understanding of *homeostasis,* the innate tendency of systems to maintain equilibrium by opposing changes that are seen to move them away from equilibrium.* Upon

---

*See George Leonard's book *Mastery* (1992), in which he discusses how the universal phenomenon known as *homeostasis* immediately raises invisible barriers to any new behavior by working to maintain all of our systems (body, mind, spirit) in equilibrium,

seeing a spotted fawn emerge tentatively from the forest, any reactive sound or speech results in the fawn quickly vanishing. In a similar way, the contemplative, upon experiencing glimpses of the supersensible, should avoid talking about them and even refrain from the attempt to "put the experience in words." This can all too easily result in the loss of the supersensible apparition.

(**cont.**) to keep things "as they are"; but in trying to keep things static, this propensity works *against* our own attempts to make what we believe to be positive changes (such as trying to eat less, or to begin a new exercise, or to sit down and meditate).

3

The Four Domains
of the Human Being

In approaching any new subject, especially one concerning invisible phenomena, it is especially useful at the outset to acquire a conceptual framework of the fundamentals. Within such a framework, related information can be organized and connections discerned to classify basic elements until they can be more fully grasped and the larger pattern understood. For Steiner, one of these conceptual frameworks can be seen in his view of the human being as existing simultaneously in each of four domains.

In *The Evolution of Consciousness,* Steiner tells us that "for higher knowledge the human being consists of four members: physical body, etheric or formative-forces body, astral body, and Ego-organization."[1]

Domain 1	Domain 2	Domain 3	Domain 4
Physical	Etheric	Astral	"I"

Fig. 3.1. Steiner's four domains of the human being.

In order to follow Steiner's instruction regarding the development of supersensible sense organs, it is essential to acquire a clear understanding of the four regions, or domains, perceived by Steiner, these being differentiable yet interpenetrating domains of the human being.

PSYCHOPHYSICS OF THE FOUR DOMAINS

To clarify the distinction among Steiner's four domains, we begin by examining their ranges in terms of what is known from *psychophysics*.* Psychophysics regards radiant energy itself as operationally manifesting in four distinct domains or modes, as shown in the table of figure 3.2, which illustrates the link between Steiner's model and modern psychophysics.

Steiner's Four Domains of a Human Being	Locus of Four Ranges of Human Energy according to Psychophysics
Ego or "I"	Radiant energy plasma— Nondual frequency domain (Bohm's implicate order)
Astral body	Magnetic energy activity— Blood plasma (Pribram's quantum brain dynamics)
Etheric body	Electrical energy activity— Nervous system (Brain and central nervous system)
Physical body	Molecular energy structure— (Organic chemistry in space-time and biochemical processes)

Fig. 3.2. Physics of the four domains.
Adapted in part from Steiner, An Occult Physiology,
and Joye, "The Pribram-Bohm Holoflux Theory."

---

*Psychophysics: The physics of perceptual systems; signal-detection system experiments using mathematics and physics. Gustav Theodor Fechner (1801–1887), who was sixty when Steiner was born, is the acclaimed "father of psychophysics." Like Steiner, this nineteenth-century scientist took an affirmatively participatory approach to the study of consciousness in the human being and was the first to publish a book applying mathematics in the modeling of perception (see *Elements of Psychophysics* [1860] 1966). Among psychologists, it is commonplace to glorify Fechner as the first user of the experimental method in the field of psychology.

THE PHYSICAL

This is the domain in which vibrating energy resonates in orderly geometric alignment. In this configuration, electromagnetic energy manifests macroscopically as particle, atom, organic or inorganic molecule, galactic cluster, liver, spleen, brain, and the seemingly infinite variety of complex semipermanent geometrical systems that manifest as the human body, the biosphere, and the lithosphere of Gaia.

In a 1911 series of lectures Steiner describes the physical on a more mundane level as it relates specifically to the human being. Steiner describes the physical as the foundation and material framework for operation of the etheric and astral domains in his model of the human being. He emphasizes that the physical domain comprises all of the systems for "the actual process of nutrition and depositing of substances," which, among others, include the biological systems responsible for secretion, excretion, nourishment, and evacuation.[2]

Modern physical science deals almost exclusively with phenomena observable in this physical realm of space and time. Scientific exploration of the physical domain has resulted in extensive medical knowledge and the technical development of innumerable physical devices we now take for granted in our "wired world." But researchers in the physical sciences have largely ignored the suggestion that consciousness itself may interact with and influence the physical world. Previously respected professionals have found themselves ostracized for exploring beyond the boundaries of their fields of physical science as currently defined, and those who would explore without the backing and funding of a scientific establishment find that much exploration has even become prohibited by law.

A clear example of such overt professional censorship exhibited by the physical-science establishment can be seen in the treatment of William A. Tiller, who studied engineering physics as a young man and rose to become a highly respected professor, researcher, and chairman of the Department of Materials Science and Engineering at Stanford University. In 1992, Cambridge University Press published Tiller's comprehensive textbook, *The Science of Crystallization*.[3] The book received high acclaim and for several decades was used as a primary engineering textbook in crystallography in universities throughout the world. In 1992, Tiller was honored with the rank of Professor Emeritus in Materials Science by Stanford, and appointed Physics Fellow of the American Association for the Advancement of Science.

During his many years of laboratory work, however, Tiller had noticed an unusual series of anomalies, results that could only be obtained if there were some unaccounted-for energy at work influencing, and even at times directing, the crystallization process. He slowly came to the conclusion that energy associated with the conscious intent of those in the laboratory might be directly interacting with the crystalline growth processes being observed. However, when Tiller began to shift some of his research time and resources into a new series of experiments designed to detect, measure, and quantify these effects, which he termed "psychoenergetic phenomena," he found that both his university support as well as his prior avenues for publishing his results were suddenly cut off. In 1997, he was unable to find a publisher for his new book, *Science and Human Transformation: Subtle Energies, Intentionality, and Consciousness* (Pavior, 1997), and was only able to interest a small New Age publishing house in this book. Since then he has written several additional books but has been unable to find a mainstream technical publisher or journal willing to accept his more recent works, such as *Psychoenergetic Science* (Pavior, 2007).

In some ways the story of William A. Tiller parallels that of Rudolf Steiner, who himself was a highly trained academic, well-versed in the sciences of his time, but whose exploration of supersensible dimensions precluded the publication of his work in scientific journals. Nevertheless, Steiner, owing to his energetic nonstop series of lectures throughout Europe, was soon able to publish and disseminate his ideas widely, beginning in the early 1900s. And like Tiller, Steiner was particularly interested in the intersection of psychic energy and the physical structure of matter and human tissue. In this area his work focused on nutrition, exercise, sports, and physical education.

Many of his ideas are currently being applied worldwide in the system of Waldorf private schools. However, in order to focus on supersensible perception, Steiner's comments on the physical domain will not be examined in detail, but rather we will focus on his discussion of the three nonphysical domains of each individual human:

- the etheric
- the astral, and
- the "I"

THE ETHERIC

The name *etheric body* is derived from the *ether,* a luminiferous, hypothetical substance through which electromagnetic waves were once thought to travel. In 1925, the Science Group of the Theosophical Research Centre in London published a work that was basically a summary of work by Annie Besant and C. W. Leadbeater. The book, *The Etheric Double,* compiled by A. E. Powell, describes the etheric body as follows:

> The correct Hindu name for the Etheric Double is *Prānamāyakosha,* or vehicle of *Prāna*: in German it is known as the "Doppelgänger.". . .
>
> Every solid, liquid and gaseous particle of the physical body is surrounded with an etheric envelope. . . .
>
> . . . It acts as an intermediary or bridge between the dense physical body and the astral body, transmitting the consciousness of physical sense-contacts through the etheric brain to the astral body, and also transmitting consciousness from the astral and higher levels down into the physical brain and nervous system.[4]

Realizing that the nervous system and physical brain manifest a flow of electrical energy conducted by nerve fibers throughout the body, the assertion can be made that the etheric body consists of this "flow" or energy matrix of electrical energy, abetted by millions of electrical pulses from firing neurons as these impulses flow along and within the neuronal pathways and between the synapses of the physical body's nervous system.

In the etheric body the primary consciousness is a time-based reflective one. Our modern human ego includes memory storage and the ability to call up memories, compare multiple memories, and apply logic to them. It includes all of the activities that we usually identify with our "self." This small self or ego might be seen alternatively as nothing more than a very powerful laptop computer running on electricity. Putting the laptop into "sleep mode" releases awareness from the etheric into the next level (the astral), in which, untrained and undeveloped, the human consciousness wanders in a world dimly recalled as "dreams."

The etheric body can thus be seen as our sophisticated machinelike ego that manifests what we take to be ourselves as human beings. Yet on this level we are basically self-captured within the electrical system of the brain, spinal cord, and distributed nervous system network. Our consciousness remains primarily within this etheric body, which, for the psychonaut, entheogenic traveler, or contemplative explorer of consciousness, is viewed as an outpost (or jumping off point) for the much deeper levels attained when the center of gravity of consciousness is able to shift toward the astral body and even beyond the astral, toward the innermost "I" at the very center, bottom, or ground of being.

Steiner points out that the etheric body, the nervous system, has been designed to deal with external perceptions: visions with their unique color, form, and brightness variation; and sounds with their complex pitch and loudness. It is within the astral body, however, that supersensible perception is to be developed, and thus it is to this next level, the astral body, that Steiner directs the initial development of the typical modern human being who seeks to acquire supersensible perception.

As suggested in figure 3.3, on page 36, Steiner's primary physical domains of the human being can be viewed as forming a rising arc of consciousness in which the physical, etheric, and astral domains are in continual two-way communication with higher levels of consciousness that themselves operate as pure radiance.

Fig. 3.3. The rising arc of consciousness.
Adapted from Steiner, An Occult Physiology.

THE ASTRAL

Steiner refers to the third level or domain of the human being as the astral body. The term *astral* (from the Greek ἄστρον for "star," "sun," "constellation"), widely used by Neoplatonists (third century CE), is found at the end of Plato's *Republic,* where he recounts the myth of Er. In the dialogue, a fallen hero suddenly revives just as he is about to be burned on a funeral pyre after appearing to be dead for twelve days. He tells of his experience traveling through seven planetary spheres that, Plato tells us, lead eventually to reincarnation, and he says that he has discovered in this journey that only the part of a human being that is "starry," or *astral,* remains after death.[5]

In the fifth century CE, Proclus, who was a lawyer in Constantinople, published an elaborate exposition of Neoplatonism. He described two subtle "planes," "bodies," or "carriers" intermediate between the individual physical human body and the immortal spirit: one carrier, the astral vehicle, was the immortal part of the soul, while the second carrier, which he considered mortal and not surviving after death, he aligned with the breath (*pneuma*).[6] It is clear that if we consider his first carrier to be Steiner's "astral" domain, then the second carrier described by Proclus must correspond with Steiner's "etheric" domain.

The table in figure 3.4 offers a comparison of the terminology that Plato, Patañjali, Proclus, and Steiner use in their writing when describing the four domains or levels of a human being.

	Domain 1	Domain 2	Domain 3	Domain 4
Steiner (20th c. CE)	Physical (Crystalline)	Etheric (Mental)	Astral (Feeling)	"I" (Immortal)
Proclus (5th c. CE)	Physical	Thought Flow	Astral	Spirit
Patañjali (4th c. CE)	Prāṇamaya Kosha	Manomaya Kosha	Vijñānamaya Kosha	Ānanadamaya Kosha
	Physical Body: Breath	Mental Body: Thought	Astral Body: Intuition	Bliss Body: Touch
Plato (4th c. BCE)	Physical Body	Nervous System	Astral/Starry Body	Immortal Spirit

Fig. 3.4. Four levels: Steiner, Proclus, Patañjali, Plato. Adapted from Steiner, An Occult Physiology; *Chlup,* Proclus: An Introduction; *Whicher,* The Integrity of the Yoga Darśana; *and Bloom,* The Republic of Plato.

MAX HEINDEL AND THE ASTRAL PLANE

Four years younger than Steiner, Max Heindel (1865–1919) was a mystic and occultist trained originally as an engineer, but who subsequently founded the esoteric belief system known as the Rosicrucian Fellowship. Born in Demark, Heindel immigrated to California in 1903, quickly became involved with C. W. Leadbeater, and only a year later was elected vice president of the Theosophical Society in Los Angeles. But Heindel was not completely happy with the theosophical approach to what he considered to be a spiritual science. The Theosophists took their teachings primarily from the Asian religious philosophies of yoga and Buddhism, whereas Heindel felt the science should not primarily focus on Asian philosophies but should include interpretations of Christian principles. Thus, in 1905, he resigned as vice president and left the Theosophical Society. Soon after, he left his engineering career behind to offer a series of lecture tours, beginning in San Francisco, in order to share what he believed to be his unique, scientifically informed understanding of occult knowledge and to explain to interested Americans how they might be able to connect with the normally invisible dimensions of the occult world.

In 1907, shortly after the end of a highly successful series of lectures in the Midwest, Heindel was invited to Berlin to speak, and while there he had the chance to attend a series of lectures by Steiner. Heindel was so astounded by the similarity between Steiner's description of the non-physical world and his own experience that he excitedly requested a private meeting with Steiner shortly after the second lecture. This resulted in a long private discussion and exchange of theories and experiences between the two men. The evening after his second private meeting with Steiner, Heindel was taken completely by surprise when he discovered, during silent meditation in his hotel room, that he had made a breakthrough into a new mode of seeing with eyes shut and awareness focused within. Suddenly, he was able to perceive and to explore new dimensions of the astral plane that he had heretofore sensed only very dimly, if at all.

Apparently, the immediate presence of Steiner had given Heindel a significant boost in his ability to "tune in" to the spirit world; upon return to Los Angeles, he began writing enthusiastically to share his new discoveries with the general public. In 1909, Heindel published his 700-page magnum opus, correlating science with religion, which he named *The Rosicrucian Cosmo-Conception*. In the same year, Heindel founded the Rosicrucian Fellowship in Oceanside, California, which later became known as "An International Association of Christian Mystics."

It is interesting to note that in the first edition of this book, Heindel published a dedication to Rudolf Steiner and included the subtitle *Occult Science*. However, in subsequent editions of the book, the dedication to Steiner was removed and the subtitle itself changed from *Occult Science* to *Mystic Christianity*. Heindel felt that too many of Steiner's pronouncements on the spirit world were spurious and misleading, and in particular where Steiner described his communications with Gautama Buddha, Jesus, and the archangel Michael. Highly suspicious of such esoteric pronouncements, Heindel criticized Steiner, stating that "what he was doing was not appropriate for America where pragmatism and clear linear thinking is predominant."[7] Indeed, Heindel asserted that he was more interested in his own, more pragmatic approach to describing the phenomena of the spirit world, as can be seen in this description of his experiential observation of the astral body:

> It is said to appear to spiritual sight as an ovoid cloud extending from sixteen to twenty inches beyond the physical body. It has a number of whirling vortices (chakras) and from the main vortex, in the region of the liver, there is a constant flow which radiates and returns. It exhibits colors that vary in every person according to his or her temperament and mood. However, the astral body (or "Soul body") must be evolved by means of the work of transmutation and will eventually be evolved by humanity as a whole.[8]

According to Heindel, the term *astral body* was employed by medieval alchemists because of its ability to confer the power to traverse the "starry" regions, and may also be the fabled Philosophers' Stone (*lapis philosophorum*) referenced in alchemical texts.[9]

BLOOD AND NERVOUS SYSTEM: ASTRAL AND ETHERIC

Physiologically, Steiner differentiates the activity of the astral from the etheric through their carriers. He senses the astral within the blood circulatory system and the etheric in the nervous system.

A ninety-degree geometric relationship between the two is stressed by Steiner in his discussion of human duality in *An Occult Physiology*, where he gives us a description, replete with diagrams, of how "nerve-activity" is at right angles to the alignment of the "blood-tablet."[10]

This description accords well with the established physical geometries of the electric field and the magnetic field, the two components of the electromagnetic field that are always at a ninety-degree angle to one another (fig. 3.5, page 40).

Human blood flow generates a strong magnetic field. This magnetic plasma is composed of hydrogen ions and heated water molecules flowing in a complex vortex of blood plasma around every cell and

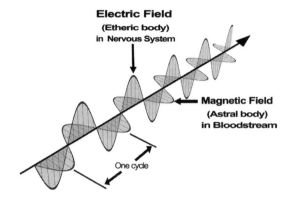

Electric Field
(Etheric body)
in Nervous System

Magnetic Field
(Astral body)
in Bloodstream

One cycle

Fig. 3.5.
Structure of the
electromagnetic
field.

through every capillary of the body. The magnetic field created by the flow of this hot ionized plasma within the circulatory system is at right angles to the electric field created by the flow of electrons along the nerves generated by firing neuron synapses.

This right-angle geometry separates the etheric from the astral, allowing the two modes of consciousness to operate independently. The contemplative psychonaut develops skills to control each of them independently. After discussing this ninety-degree relationship of consciousness between nerves and blood, Steiner gives us another key for further development of supersensory perception.

> It is, therefore, possible purely through processes of inner concentration, to separate the blood-system from the nerve-system. . . . Now, the peculiar thing is that when the human being once actually brings this about through such inward exertion of the soul, he has then an entirely different sort of inner experience. . . . When, through inner concentration, he separates his nerve-system, lifts it, that is to say, through inner soul-forces out of his blood-system, he does not then live in his ordinary ego but another Self. . . . He feels a supersensible world uplifted within him.[11]

It is through practice of "inner concentration," Steiner says, that one gradually develops the skills to be able to bring deep silence to the mental chatter of the nervous system. At this point one begins to sense the supersensible in the bloodstream.

QUANTUM BRAIN DYNAMICS: AN ASTRAL PLANE

Recent research in neurophysiology provides new support for Steiner's perception of a special region of consciousness operating within the human blood circulatory system. In recent years researchers in the field of quantum brain dynamics (QBD) have concluded that distributed consciousness, the sense of self termed "I," is to be found, not primarily within the neuronal system of nerves or the specific organ of the brain, but within the liquid volume of the hydrogen-ionized bloodstream plasma that fills the human circulatory system.[12]

Modern physiologists and neuroscientists tacitly assume that consciousness can be associated *only* with the nervous system and the brain. Over a century ago Gustav Fechner fought against this same assumption, which he called the "nerve issue." Fechner addresses this assumption with some amusing analogies.

> Since violins need strings to sound, then flutes also need strings; but since flutes have no strings, they cannot sound; candles and petroleum lamps need wicks in order to burn, so gas lamps also need wicks, but they have none; thus they cannot burn. Yet flutes sound without strings and gas lamps burn without wicks. . . . If fish and worms can breathe without having lungs, while mammals and birds can breathe only if they have lungs, why cannot plants without nerves experience perception, while animals can only perceive when they do have nerves?[13]

In 1995, the Japanese neurophysiologists Mari Jibu and Kunio Yasue described the creation and annihilation dynamics of units of concrescing consciousness, which they characterized as *quanta* of consciousness, and linked these quanta to the physical properties of water, stating that they are "energy quanta of the water rotational field extending to the whole assembly of brain cells, and photons, that is, energy quanta of the electromagnetic field."[14]

Jibu and Yasue go on to describe a theory in which the polarization of water molecules plays an exceptional part and on the macro level produces a single resonant water "macromolecule" in bodies of living, water-based creatures. Within this nonlocal quantum field (that is generated throughout the human circulatory system) is embedded an electromagnetic field in the form of an ionized blood plasma* vortex. That our blood acts as a plasma should not be surprising, as the first line in Francis Chen's highly regarded textbook on plasma physics reads: "It has often been said that 99% of the matter in the universe is in the plasma state."

Through applying quantum brain mechanics, Jibu and Yasue show how the consciousness of a living organism can be viewed as equivalent to "the unity of water" in the human body, or as "a single molecule" of consciousness within the human blood stream.

> There are two basic fields in quantum brain dynamics (QBD): the water rotational field and the electromagnetic field. The two must be described simultaneously by quantum field theory because they interact with each other. . . . All H_2O molecules bound together in a QBD vacuum domain form a single, extensive molecule of water in a macroscopic domain. That is, water throughout the entire region of the cerebral cortex is thought to be composed of many macroscopic water molecules whose sizes are all comparable to the coherence length of the QBD vacuum, that is, about 50 microns. This remarkable feature of water in living matter might provide us with quantum field theoretical support for the idea that life is nothing but the unity of water as a single molecule in living matter.[15]

---

*Plasma is a state of matter in which a significant portion of the particles are ionized. Plasmas are by far the most common phase of matter in the universe, both by mass and by volume. All stars are made of plasma, and interstellar space is filled with plasma. Common forms of plasma include lightning, St. Elmo's fire, the polar auroras, the solar wind, neon signs, and plasma displays in modern televisions. See Francis F. Chen, *Introduction to Plasma Physics and Controlled Fusion*, vol. 1, *Plasma Physics*, 56.

This observation from quantum brain dynamics supports Steiner's model of an astral body of consciousness beyond the etheric body of the nervous system and brain. The supporting pattern can be seen in the QBD manifestation of a "single, extensive molecule of water," dipolar in geometry like an antenna, generating a complex magnetic field through the circulation of the hot hydrogen ions of blood plasma.

Thus, we find existing within the blood system of the human body an extensively polarized "super cell" of magnetic energy that can be identified as Steiner's astral body of consciousness,* as differentiated from the etheric body of consciousness that itself is generated by electrical activity in the nervous system.

This astral body, a magnetic component of the blood, is in the human being largely outside of the range of the consciousness of the etheric activity in the electrical neuronal system during waking states of human consciousness. But as we have seen, Steiner tells us that "it is, therefore, possible purely through processes of inner concentration, to separate the blood-system from the nerve-system."[16]

Thus, there is system of dual consciousness in the human being, one operating largely within the electrical activity of the nervous system and brain, and the second mode of consciousness operational in the dipolar magnetic blood plasma.

> As human beings, we actually stand in the world as a duality, a duality
> in the first place which has, in the nervous system of the brain and the
> spinal cord, instruments that bring external impressions to the blood.[17]

Additional support for this view can be found more recently in the research conclusions of Rollin McCraty, head of HeartMath Institute in California, who summarizes an essay describing his research findings with the following:

> In conclusion, I believe that the electromagnetic energy generated by
> the heart is an untapped resource within the human system awaiting

---

*This is also the same "astral body" as identified by Plato, Proclus, and Patañjali.

further exploration and application. Acting as a synchronizing force within the body, a key carrier of emotional information, and an apparent mediator of a type of subtle electromagnetic communication between people, the cardiac bioelectromagnetic field may have much to teach us about the inner dynamics of health and disease as well as our interactions with others.[18]

"I": THE ONE AND ONLY REAL "EGO"

But even beyond the human being's existence within the nervous system's electrical (etheric) and the bloodstream's magnetic (astral) dimensional ranges of energy, Steiner insists that "we must give birth to a new, higher being within us," and that through developing the astral we find that "something comes to life in us that transcends the personal or individual."[19] This is where the fourth realm, or fourth state, enters the picture. In classical Indian philosophy the term *turiya* is Sanskrit for "fourth" and identified with the highest stage of human consciousness. Steiner's fourth mode of consciousness is that which is perceived actively via the heart during supersensible perception (psychonautics in an ocean of psychic entities).

In discussing this highest goal of the human psyche, Steiner also refers to it with the terms "Ego," and "I," but in a particular way and not as commonly understood. Steiner's "Ego" and "I" refer not to the "little I" and "little ego" habitually active within the etheric body of socialized human beings. The little ego is, to a great extent, the product of the wiring of the human nervous system laid down by DNA encoding and of memory storage, as in a laptop computer, with the sequential electronic activity that gives rise to the avatar of an ego that is active in most humans between states of sleep, molded by a lifetime of experience and memory. This individual ego is the one explored and dealt with by modern psychology and psychiatry (Carl Jung excepted), not the Ego, the "I" referred to by Steiner. That higher Ego of Steiner, referenced by Jung as the Self, has through the ages been discovered, experienced, and documented by a rare few human beings spanning innumerable cultures. Documented accounts reveal the experiences of those who have attained to this fourth state of consciousness, whether from drugs, contemplative practices, or natural ability. From this higher dimensional perspective, many have been able to interact with entities variously called spirits, angels, guides, or aliens. Others have been able to converse with those who have passed beyond.

Steiner urges us to "go into the silence" in order for the organs of supersensible perception to awaken. As we enter the silence, the etheric (electrical) activity associated with memory, words, and logical process-ing is reduced to a minimum. Inner perceptions of touch associated with the astral (magnetic) begin to emerge more clearly into awareness. At this point Steiner urges us to continue beyond etheric thinking and astral feeling, to pass through what he strikingly terms "the zero-point of silence" into a new world of awareness, the fourth dimension.

> There would be not only the absolute peace of the zero-point of silence but it would go further and come to the negative of hear-ing, quieter than quiet, more silent than silence. And this must in fact happen when we are able through enhanced powers to reach this inner peace and silence. When, however, we arrive at this inner negative of audibility, at this peace greater than the zero-point of peace, we are then so deeply in the spiritual world that we not only see it but hear it resounding.[20]

What we are "hearing" when we have penetrated this zero-point of silence are not the familiar audible sound vibrations from the external world, but sensations of resonance-touch trilling in the blood. We dis-cover we are beginning to sense a high energy web of vibratory energy flowing and intercommunicating in multiple networks both within our body and throughout the cosmos. We have reached the fourth domain of the human being, the Ānandamaya Kosha, the Bliss Body of Patañjali, the Immortal Spirit described by Plato. In the next chapter we will explore various techniques to facilitate our efforts to achieve this state of supersensible awareness.

4

Conditions for
Supersensible Perception

In his book *Knowledge of the Higher Worlds* Steiner describes, in a chapter called "Some Practical Aspects," numerous ways in which we can facilitate the acquisition of supersensible perception. Among these are included, of course, patience and perseverance, but also the cultivation of an enduring mode of gentleness with ourselves (even more so than with others) and development of the skill of nonattachment to anger by catching it before it arises. In teachings for advanced practitioners, Steiner counsels being fully open to both the love and the suffering that one will experience as one enters a life in which new ranges of supersensible perception and supersensible sensation are opening.

And not only attitudinal conditions but external conditions can be conducive to acquiring supersensible perception. The environment can be extremely important.

> Especially fortunate is the student who can carry out his esoteric training surrounded by the green world of plants, or among the sunny hills, where nature weaves her web of sweet simplicity. This environment develops the inner organs in a harmony which can never ensue in a modern city.[1]

However, even city dwellers, cut off from "the pines and snow peaks," can persevere and make progress through practice, as "there are many ways to the summit of insight."[2] But above all, Steiner urges, it is patience that is requisite at every stage in order that one continues to persevere daily in practice and seeking. He describes someone who has this experience as follows:

> He has persevered patiently for years without any marked result. Suddenly, while silently seated in his quiet chamber, spiritual light envelops him; the walls disappear, become transparent for his soul, and a new world expands before his eyes that have become seeing, or resounds in his ears that have become spiritually hearing.[3]

FASHIONING ORGANS
OF HIGHER PERCEPTION

Steiner's teaching includes numerous practices and exercises that are found in all religions and mystical teachings. The student is requested to develop "a quality of gentleness"[4] and to learn to overcome and master the eruption of anger, which clouds the mind, shielding it from the sensitivities needed for supersensible perception. With this quality of gentleness, the student will begin to perceive "all the subtleties in the soul-life of his environment."[5] Steiner describes the technique of entering "the silence," much like Patañjali's "stilling of the changing states" of the mind.

> Persevere in silent inner seclusion; close the senses to all that they brought you before your training; reduce to absolute immobility all the thoughts which, according to your previous habits, surged within you; become quite still and silent within, wait in patience, and then the higher worlds will begin to fashion and perfect the organs of sight and hearing in your soul and spirit.[6]

ENTERING THE SILENCE:
LOVE AND SUFFERING

Having sufficiently attained to a state of inner silence, the practitioner begins to experience the arising of intuitive thinking. There soon occurs a rupture of plane,* a passage from one cosmic domain to another, at which point one begins the exploration of a supersensible universe. These perceptions can result in ranges and intensities of emotional experience previously unknown, says Steiner.

> You feel the suffering on which the whole existence of the world is founded, and this suffering is at the same time a loneliness; nothing yet is there. But the capacity for love, flowing up from within in manifold forms, leads you on to enter with your own being into all that now appears visibly, audibly, as Inspiration. Through this capacity for love you enter first into one spiritual Being, then into another . . . these Beings of the higher Hierarchies—we now learn to live in our experience of them.[7]

That it is a good sign when tears begin to well up during contemplative practice has been corroborated by Saint Isaac the Syrian, a seventh-century contemplative mystic living on the eastern shores of what is now Saudi Arabia.

> Though you should suspend yourself by your eyelids before God, do not think you have attained to anything by the manner of life which you lead until you have attained to tears. For until then, your hidden self is in the service of the world; that is, you are leading the life of those who dwell in the world, and do the work of God with the outward man. But the inward man is still without fruit, for his fruit begins with tears. When you attain to the region of tears, then know that your mind has left the prison of this world and has set its foot on the journey to the new age, and has begun to breathe that other air, new and wonderful. And at the same moment it begins to shed tears, since the birth pangs of the spiritual infant are at hand.[8]

---

*A "rupture of plane," also termed a "rent in the fabric of being" (by the historian of religion Mircea Eliade), allows the powers native to one domain to briefly manifest themselves in another. See Michael Washburn, *Embodied Spirituality in a Sacred World,* 52.

THE TASK AHEAD

Steiner has given us detailed techniques on the acquisition of supersensible perception, something that is, he claims, achievable by contemporary human beings. One of the primary techniques he stresses recurrently is one that is virtually identical with the ancient Indian yoga method taught by Patañjali: to practice deep silence, to quiet the mind. In Steiner's model, the etheric mind, or in psychophysical terms, the neuronal electrical nervous system activity, must be controlled sufficiently to be attenuated, suspended, made quiet. With practice the human biocomputer[9] can learn how to suspend the various subsystems involved in the thinking and remembering activity of the etheric, neuroelectrical mind.

The silence thus ensuing will allow pure perceptual consciousness to shift from neurons into the blood, the magnetic mode of the astral consciousness of the dipolar blood plasma, permitting resonance with the geo-magnetosphere and opening multiple avenues for interacting with energies of a magnetic nature.

At this point begins the development of the organs of supersensible perception. The seeker directs the attention of the astral to the locations within the body in which reside these inner organs, corresponding roughly to the location of chakras described in texts and diagrams of Indian yoga. Each one of these several organs of supersensible perception operates within a different range of energy, a different bandwidth, a different dimensional space, says Steiner: "It must be clearly understood that the perceptions of each single organ . . . bear a different character . . . [and] transmit quite different perceptions."[10]

Yet even beyond this astral realm with its inner organs of supersensible perception, even beyond the magnetic bandwidth of the ionized dipolar blood plasma, Steiner tells us, lies a higher Ego in a nontemporal zero-point silence, and it is toward this that Steiner directs his students as the ultimate goal: knowledge of the one true Self, the higher Ego. It is the attainment of centering within this higher Ego, which is to be found beyond ordinary waking ego awareness, that must be the goal of each human being, and Steiner tells us that this is achievable with regular effort and patience.

Our task, then, is to give birth, within us, to a higher state of being. At first this is difficult because never does a dominant and dominating system like the individual electric ego of the brain and nervous system easily consent to relinquish control, to let go sufficiently to share power with an alternate domain, even of a higher configuration. Out of self-preservation the little ego does not want to be shut down nor allow itself to be bypassed as consciousness begins to shift and tune beyond the etheric of the nervous system, moving into the astral consciousness of the bloodstream, and begins to resonate more fully within the fourth realm, that of the Ego, that of the real and immortal "I."

Acting on this inherent urge for self-preservation, the little ego responds defensively. Thus initial experiences of one's true Self are often accompanied by a great sense of insecurity, even fear. The twentieth century contemplative Edward Salim Michael (1921–2006) vividly describes feelings frequently associated with this first encounter.

> When looked at from one's habitual level of being, this out-of-the-ordinary aspect of one's nature into which one merges and becomes transformed during deep meditation *is* a sort of insecurity, in the sense that, at that moment, one is completely cut off from all that one had been familiar with, so mentally and physically habituated toward and so utterly dependent upon to feel oneself. It is, in a way, understandable that some people may in the beginning feel lost or insecure at such times. For this unusual state of being and of consciousness is, to begin with, related to the hitherto totally unknown experience of a strange inner Universe and a most curious feeling of vast cosmic "Aloneness." And even the feeling of infinity, as well as the profound stillness, that descend upon them and pervade their being at such moments may, at first, create a sensation of immense awe and apprehension if they are not prepared.[11]

In reacting to this common fear-based insecurity, it is useful to cling

to the remembrance that "this too will pass," and indeed it will in a relatively short time. While waiting for such negative feeling to dissipate it is
beneficial to silently verbalize a prayer, a mantra, or a memorized poem,
abiding patiently until the feelings of insecurity pass and one becomes
more accustomed to the sensation of having shifted the center of gravity
of consciousness away from the "little ego" to the greater "Self."

In this chapter we have examined practical methods found in
Steiner's *Knowledge of the Higher Worlds,* in which we have seen the
utility of viewing each human being as functioning simultaneously
on four very different levels. These four modes or bandwidths of the
human each need to be developed and tuned, but even more importantly, they must be trained to communicate and coordinate with each
other and with the much deeper inner Self.

We have seen that it is through the physical realm or level that we
eat, secrete, multiply, move, and sense the world. It is within the domain
of the second level, the etheric, that our "little ego" thinks, stores and
retrieves memories, and processes the sensations brought to the nervous
system from the physical sensory organs. In a real way our physical bodies and neurophysical systems operate as avatars of the real Self, which
is beyond normal cognition. And then there is the third level of human
awareness, the astral field, felt as a magnetic sensation of energy that
is pulling inwardly, perpendicular to the etheric field. This flowing
magnetic flux resonates within our blood plasma as felt emotion. It is
through resonance with this magnetic astral region that we feel, broadcast, and receive direct emotive information from the hearts of other
living beings as well as from more ethereal beings at other levels of existence in the biosphere of our planet and the outer (and inner) reaches of
the cosmos. It is this astral world that is the first goal in our efforts to
develop supersensible perception.

And yet there is yet a further goal even beyond the astral, a fourth
level of being beyond the electrical brain, the magnetic blood, the material systems of energy that manifest our existence. This fourth dimension or level is experienced as a leap into the beyond-zero silence of the
eternal Ego, the One True Self.

5

My Journey from Physics to Metaphysics

While the conditions for supersensible perception may have been set during my childhood through focus on Mesmer's tactics for hypnotizing my friends and subsequent efforts to develop "animal magnetism" by contemplating a candle flame, it was definitely the experience of entheogens during the summer of 1967 that finally established my long-range personal and career goals.

This unexpected deeper experience of consciousness began around a small campfire on a lovely Pacific Ocean beach just south of Big Sur, California, at around midnight on a clear July night, shortly after ingesting three small yellow tablets of LSD-25 ("Owsley acid"). Having just completed a spring term of mathematics and electrical engineering (as well as an English Romantic poetry course), my vision of the universe was deeply influenced by such things as frequency charts and the mathematics of the Fourier transforms, electromagnetic theories describing invisible energy waves, and Greek nature gods. Suddenly, all of these dry paradigms became vividly alive for me, overlaid and energized with the direct visual, auditory, and tactile experience of other entities in an enormous sea of energy. Astonished, I found myself floating on the vast depths of oceans of consciousness that I had never noticed, lying beyond the shores of my own familiar mind, and I suddenly realized that we (meaning everyone and every single thing) are all immersed in planetary and galactic fields of energy swirling in and out of our own limited islands of awareness.

Several years later, in a book written by the medical psychonaut* John Cunningham Lilly (1915–2001), a physician, neuroscientist, psychoanalyst, philosopher, writer, and inventor, I came across a description that resonated intensely with my recollections of "what it was like" under LSD. Here Lilly briefly describes his own initial experience with LSD while floating in body-temperature water in one of his carefully designed lightproof, soundproof isolation tanks.

> I am a small point of consciousness in a vast domain beyond my understanding. Vast forces of the evolution of the stars are whipping me through colored streamers of light becoming matter, matter becoming light. The atoms are forming from light, light is forming from the atoms. A vast consciousness directs these huge transitions.
>
> With difficulty I maintain my identity, my self. The surrounding processes interpenetrate my being and threaten to disrupt my own integrity, my continuity in time. There is no time; this is an eternal place, with eternal processes generated by beings far greater than I. I become merely a small thought in that vast mind that is practically unaware of my existence. I am a small program in the huge cosmic computer. There is no existence, no being but *this* forever. There is no place to go back to. There is no future, no past, but *this*.[1]

My own experiences under the influence of LSD-25 had opened my eyes to a completely new paradigm of what it might mean to exist on this planet, among the stars, as a "conscious being." Something had suddenly thrown wide open the shutters of the universe; no longer could I regard the real world in the relatively constricted ranges I had inherited from previous generations, which I had unquestioningly adopted as the boundaries of reality.

---

*The methodology for exploring and mapping subjectively those regions of consciousness communed with during altered states of consciousness (holotropic states), including states induced by meditation, contemplative techniques, entheogenic substances, prayer, or physical exercise; direct exploration involves a psychonaut developing the capacity to voluntarily attenuate mental ego activity while maintaining focus on detected resonances from the "whole," "I," or "Self," both immanent and transcendent.

While I was able to continue in my role as an engineering student, completing my engineering program the following year, the intense psychonautic experiences on the beach at night in the ocean of consciousness had kindled a flame of enthusiasm for exploring and understanding consciousness as a phenomenon in its own right. No longer was my fascination focused so exclusively on radio and laser communication theory; I found that I could not stop thinking about the word *consciousness*. I pondered what a deeper understanding of the concept might imply for my own religious practices, for prayer and for mystical experiences beyond the state of simply "being awake." Indeed, I had acquired my first taste of "psychonautics," of sailing beyond the edge of the familiar into a heretofore concealed "ocean of consciousness" within which we all exist, yet it is as invisible to us as water is to fish swimming in the ocean.

However, it was only a few months later, one October night in the Texas hill country, twenty miles from Austin, that I was confronted with even stranger phenomena than those I had experienced during my LSD-catalyzed night on the beach; a startling and unexpected apparition in the Texas forest reinforced my new fascination with trying to explore and understand the intersections of science and mysticism.

THE LIGHT IN THE FOREST

It was around midnight at a place known as Hamilton Pool, twenty miles southwest of Austin, above an ancient crack in the earth known as the Balcones Fault. Fed by a fifty-foot waterfall, the large pool of water had been created when the limestone dome over an underground cavern had collapsed due to quakes and erosion many millennia past.

Three classmates and I had come to swim after a week of final exams at the University of Texas. The night was quiet except for the chirping of small frogs, and pale clouds obscured the stars. After swimming in the deeper parts of the pool, not far from the waterfall, we soon gathered by the edge of the pool and talked quietly.

The first noticeable sign of something unusual was the abrupt cessation of the frogs' peeping, part of that incessant forest murmur of crickets and frogs on a summer night. Abruptly, they stopped, leaving only the gentle splashing sound of the waterfall across the pool from us.

Soon, a barely perceptible glow appeared far down the creek, back to our right, where the water flowed from the pool toward the Pedernales River about half a mile to the west. The light, growing and fading in rhythmic pulsations, bobbed slowly up and down along the creek, obscured by intervening pine trees and brush. We sat in silence, backs against a large boulder on the shore of Hamilton Pool, both mesmerized and nervous. We were familiar with ominous urban legends that circulated in Austin, warning of nighttime horror in the forested hill country to the west of Austin, stories of people alone in the woods at night who had mysteriously vanished, echoed some years later in the movie *The Texas Chainsaw Massacre* (1974).

At long last, emerging from the obscuring brush, what appeared to be a spherical object of pale opal phosphorescence came into view, floating high above the creek. Gently glowing and slowly pulsing, the orb majestically moved along the rim of the cliff overhanging the pool of water. After what seemed to be an eternity, the softly glowing spherical shape reached the waterfall, and after rising slightly and moving closer to the falling water, the apparition slowly dipped three times, bobbing and weaving in a stately rhythmical pattern above the water before the falls, like some gigantic moth in the night. Eventually, it resumed its motion along the sheltering rim, moving ever closer to us where we sat on the pebble-strewn beach, speechless, paralyzed, more in awe than in fear.

Finally, the apparition reached us where we sat on the shore, our backs pressed against the cool boulder. There it paused, hovering, about ten feet above us, a small, silent, spherical galaxy of tiny bright stars and glowing filaments, flashing and flickering. Within the mysterious, luminous orb could be seen patterns, like thin contrails, all bound within a sphere approximately two feet in diameter, about the size of a large beach ball. Time stood still. I held my breath, speechless, in awe verging on disbelief for what seemed an eternity. At last it began again its slow, bobbing movement away from us, continuing its journey above the beach edge until it reached the creek that drains the pool. Then it continued west, above the creek, in a slow stately fashion, moving back into the swampy forest from which it had first appeared.

What I felt and perceived beneath the apparition is difficult to recall, yet alone relate. I remember clearly hearing peculiar whistling sounds and the distinct sensation of electrical snappings of some sort in my head. At the same time, I felt an intensity of a kind I had never previously experienced. It was apparent that here, in the unbroken silence of this remote Texas countryside, far from any town or city, we had encountered a mystery beyond anything I had previously considered or discovered in any of my books.

In the following days the four of us could not stop talking about the apparition. Had we seen a UFO? Or was this the same experience of something historically referred to as a wood spirit, leprechaun, fairy, ghost, or angel? In its trajectory around the pool we all agreed it had moved with direction and intent and seemed to have displayed an awareness. It was alive, clearly, though not made of any identifiable material or substance; it had appeared as a transparent sphere, manifesting glowing electric sparks and lines in visibly changing swirls, as might be seen in holographic moiré patterns (fig. 5.1).

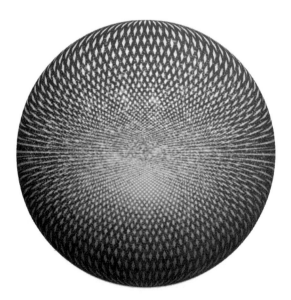

Fig. 5.1. Moiré patterns in spherical volume.

We agreed that as the sphere hovered above us the impression was one of benevolent curiosity. Could this have been some kind of machine? Its movements did not seem machinelike, but gave the impression of intelligence, particularly in the lovely "dance" it made in front of the waterfall, and later as it hovered directly above us, twinkling and glowing in pastel aurora-like colors. The sphere seemed to be considering us, observing us intently. The next morning we all agreed that we had been both terrified and amazed, and, like deer caught in car headlights, we had frozen and could neither move nor think nor react.

Many years later, I came across descriptions of similar encounters with orbs of glowing light in the writings of both John Blofeld (1913–1987)[2] and Aleister Crowley (1875–1947).[3]

Born in London in 1913, Blofeld was fascinated by Buddhism and contemplation practices from an early age. He traveled to China in 1937, spending the next decade visiting remote monasteries and sacred mountains in China, Mongolia, and Tibet. In *The Wheel of Life: The Autobiography of a Western Buddhist,* Blofeld relates that he once visited the Temple of Wutai Shan on a mountain of the same name in northern China, sacred to the bodhisattva of wisdom, Wénshū (文殊 in Chinese). Here Blofeld relates his experience one night on the top floor of a three-story meditation tower constructed on the slopes of the holy mountain of Wutai Shan.

> The ascent to the door of the tower occupied less than a minute. As each one entered the little room and came face to face with the window beyond, he gave a shout of surprise, as though all our hours of talk had not sufficiently prepared us for what we now saw. There in the great open spaces beyond the window, apparently not more than one or two hundred yards away, innumerable balls of fire floated majestically past. We could not judge their size, for nobody knew how far away they were. . . . Fluffy balls of orange colored fire, moving through space, unhurried and majestic—truly a fitting manifestation of divinity![4]

The temple was renowned for the fact that (according to the Buddhist monks there) bodhisattvas could often be seen floating down from the mountaintop in the form of spheres of light, and special meditation platforms had been constructed so that the balls could be observed by contemplatives. Blofeld continues in an attempt to categorize what he and his companions had seen that night:

> I do not know if this extraordinary sight has ever been accounted for "scientifically" and I am not much interested in such explanations. It is far lovelier to think of them as divine manifestations, however prosaic their real nature may be. But is it prosaic? Marsh gas, you say? Marsh gas right out in space, a thousand or more feet above the nearest horizontal surface and some hundreds of feet from the vertical surface of a cold, rocky mountain innocent of water? Surely not.[5]

Aleister Crowley, the English painter, theosophist, and mountaineer, recorded in his biography the details of a similar experience of a seemingly living sphere of light. He describes such a sphere entering his hut by a lake in Scotland during a violent thunderstorm. He writes that at first he thought it must be St. Elmo's fire, balls of light often seen hovering about the top masts of sailing ships during thunderstorms at sea, but the one that appeared to have entered his cottage during a storm seemed clearly to be alive as it moved in a stately procession around the room, as if studying the environment, then dashing straight toward Crowley's face, only to stop suddenly, and after what seemed to be an interminable period, moving slowly back out of the hut and vanishing into the storm.

The impact of the strikingly otherworldly apparition at Hamilton Pool on my twenty-one-year-old, recently acquired physics and electrical engineering mind-set, following that summer's LSD experience on a California beach, opened my eyes to an entirely new dimension for exploration and research. How could I have seen and experienced these things so vividly, phenomena of nature (or supernature) that were never referred to by any of the current sciences? The occurrence at Hamilton Pool had rocked my scientifically indoctrinated sensibilities, abruptly opening my eyes to a wide range of new dimensions for both scientific and experiential exploration, regions far beyond the current maps so carefully explored by physicists, biologists, and radio engineers.

IN SEARCH OF THE MIRACULOUS

Nine months later I graduated with my degree in electrical engineering and left Texas for New York, where I soon found my first job as an electrical engineer in the World Trade Center, on the sixty-fourth floor of the north tower. While I worked during the day as a design engineer, my evenings and weekends were primarily filled with efforts to expand my understanding of the phenomenon of consciousness.

Being an avid reader since an early age, I spent many Saturdays searching through the stacks of the New York Public Library in the center of Manhattan, one of the largest public libraries in the United States, second only to the Library of Congress in Washington, D.C. At the time I was searching through subject areas that dealt largely with psychology and science, hoping to find material relevant to consciousness and in particular to "out of the ordinary" experiences. One Saturday morning I noticed a book someone had left on a reading table, and I opened it and began reading. The title of the book was *In Search of the Miraculous: Fragments of an Unknown Teaching,* and I was surprised to learn that the author had been a mathematician, a Russian named Pyotr Demianovich Ouspensky (1878–1947).[6] Having always been impressed by technically credentialed writers, I checked the book out of the library and, with a mixture of awe and reverence, spent the rest of the weekend reading Ouspensky's book in my loft on Canal Street in lower Manhattan. Here I found a deep, articulate discussion of experiences and concepts that directly addressed the subject of consciousness that now so fascinated me. Up until then I had assumed that all books fell into one of two categories, technical nonfiction and fiction. Yet here was a book written by a highly trained professional mathematician, describing his experiences during a three-year exploration of consciousness and search for "the miraculous" under the guidance of his teacher, a Greek–Armenian Orthodox Christian mystic named George Ivanovich Gurdjieff. Reading the first page, I was immediately captivated, finding in Ouspensky's opening passages, word for word, a description perfectly mirroring my own search. Ouspensky writes here of his search for the miraculous:

> I had said that I was going to "seek the miraculous." The "miraculous" is very difficult to define. But for me this word had a quite definite meaning. I had come to the conclusion a long time ago that there was no escape from the labyrinth of contradictions in which we live except by an entirely new road, unlike anything hitherto known or used by us. But where this new or forgotten road began I was unable to say. I already knew then as an undoubted fact that beyond the thin film of false reality there existed another reality from which, for some reason, something separated us. The "miraculous" was a penetration into this unknown reality. And it seemed to me that the way to the unknown could be found in the East.[7]

Ouspensky's book opened my eyes to an entirely new category of writing that I had not previously imagined existed, and I suddenly realized that what I had been seeking might be found in the "esoteric" subject areas of mysticism, occultism, theosophy, and Asian philosophies; all of these were topics I had never before been introduced to in high school or university courses, as they were routinely ignored by the scientifically trained communities. Nor had the nuns who taught Sunday school ever mentioned such subjects, as their focus seems to have been restricted to church history and dogma.

In addition to suddenly "discovering" an entirely new range of reading material to be explored, I soon acquired the habit of attending various lectures and workshops dealing with meditation and the esoteric; New York in the early 1970s had become a center of activity for New Age teachers and authorities on esoteric contemplative practices, and over the next several years I was able to study with a number of seemingly authentic teachers, including Swami Satchidananda Saraswati, Chögyam Trungpa Rinpoche, John Lilly, and Alan Watts. But during my five years in New York I had no idea that there might also be rich mystical traditions and teachings within my own Christian roots, and so my focus was on absorbing theory and concepts from Buddhist, Taoist, and Hindu and psychonautic techniques from John Lilly and Alan Watts.

TUNING THE MIND

During this time I was living in a two-room flat on the fifth floor of a five-story walk-up in the Lower East Side of New York (Avenue A and East 6th Street). The neighborhood was full of Indian vegetarian restaurants and an influx of a young and noisy immigrants. How I came to live in this apartment is a story in itself. At work in the World Trade Center, I had befriended a young engineer, Rudy Israel, the only person I have ever known from Trinidad, my birthplace. For many years he had rented a fifth-floor apartment on East 6th Street in the city, where he could party with friends in privacy (he lived with his parents in Queens), but since he was getting married, he offered me the apartment. It was a strange place and a rough neighborhood at the time (gentrified now). The rent was exceedingly cheap, at $21 per month, so I decided to accept Rudy's offer.

Each floor in the building had its own social ecology. As I entered the building up the stairs from the sidewalk to the first floor, I passed an apartment that always seemed to have the door partly open and restrained with a chain, revealing a blue light coming from within and a few African Americans living there (rumored to sell drugs). The second floor housed an apartment with a Puerto Rican couple, who often sounded as if they were fighting; they were rumored to be a pimp and his girl. The third floor housed a mysterious, quiet man from Poland, who had covered his door with sheet metal. At first he would only whisper to me when greeted in the hall, acting strangely paranoid, as if someone might be spying on us. Eventually, he trusted me enough to invite me into his apartment for oolong tea. I learned that he had helped design cooling systems for MIG fighter planes under the Soviet occupation as a young engineer, but had escaped with his brother over the mountains via a cross-country skiing adventure. On the fourth floor was a very old lady who lived alone and sadly passed away during my second year there, only to be discovered a week later when the smell was detected in the hallway near her apartment. Though it was a challenge to carry heavy groceries up five flights, my apartment had the advantage of lowering most of the noise of the city neighborhood, and my innermost room was wonderfully quiet, especially at night.

One late evening I was in my quiet room doing my usual stretching exercises, trying to maintain a shoulder-stand posture (*sarvāṅgāsana*) for ten minutes as part of my hatha yoga routine. Part of the exercise was to move into the pose, then to become as quiet as possible, practicing internal silence. This required making an effort to attenuate every thought that might arise, to detach from and not follow memories as they began to form, nor to allow any inner dialogue to resume streaming. The goal was to open up the bandwidth of awareness and to remain receptive, just listening. Suddenly, out of the silence, I heard a singular, loud, high-pitched tone that seemed to be located somewhere within my cranium. I noticed that as I focused my awareness on the sound it seemed to coalesce into a point while substantially increasing in volume! I quickly feared I might be experiencing a brain aneurism in progress. But I soon discovered that by maintaining my focus, I was able to coax the sound into growing louder and more distinct, and my fears were transformed into awe at this audible tone coming from within. After several minutes of relaxing into the sound, I was surprised by a feeling of "touch" detectible at the source of the strange high-pitched frequency somewhere within the left part of my brain.

Then things became even more strange. After noticing the initial "bright" sound, additional "points" of sound of distinctly different pitch began to rise into awareness *in other locations in my cranium*. I gently lowered myself from my shoulder-stand position and, ending my yoga for the night, lay down under a blanket in the dark. For many hours that night I could not sleep as I played with the sounds in my head, amazed that I could clearly hear them increase in volume according to the degree that I was able to maintain focus upon them. I noticed, however, that as soon as I would begin consciously thinking "about them" or "thinking in words," letting my attention begin to stray, they would subside and contact would be lost. I quickly learned that by gently dropping my train of thought, which seemed so insistent on thinking, classifying, and so on, I was able once more to enter the silence, and the tiny sounds would suddenly peek out of the silence again and increase in volume in what was clearly a feedback loop, a sort of reverberation responding to my search. The tones were quite pure and high-pitched, and I suppose most people would classify them as a "ringing in the ears." Several months later I discovered the term *tinnitus,* which was defined by medical science as any perceived sound not brought in by the ear canal. Since perception of these sounds seemed to bother people, doctors decided that it must be a disease of the hearing system with an unknown (or yet to be determined) source.

Nevertheless, by now being quite serious in my efforts to explore the phenomenon of consciousness by any means possible, catalyzed by the unknown dimensions I had experienced on LSD and the Austin forest encounter with the glowing sphere of living light, I was completely fascinated by what was happening that night in my top-floor apartment. I found that by trying to ignore a particularly dominant bright sound and trying to focus on a fainter, more obscure sound ("further away from" or "behind" the first), the second sound would immediately grow louder in volume and become easier to focus on using this inner focal-sense mechanism. Here was direct cause and effect, albeit in an internal domain of consciousness among some kind of living experiential fields of energy dynamics. That night I lay awake in the dark, moving from sound to sound within my head, as each would rise and fall, almost as if each had an independent volition of its own. I experienced strong emotional oscillations between exaltation verging on disbelief and terror that I might be damaging my neuronal centers, perhaps even encouraging (or experiencing) a brain-damaging hemorrhage.

As an electrical engineer, I had often listened to various single sinusoidal tones generated by equipment in laboratory sessions, yet this was not a single tone but a confluence of tones faintly making up a background of the perceived, sensed audio range, like those aforementioned peepers in the forest at night at Hamilton Pool. It was at specific points in space within my cranium that from time to time a tone would arise with exponential sharpness high above the background level, to become a bright point, like a beacon that, if I were able to sustain focus on it for a few moments, would become markedly louder with an accompanying intense tactile sensation.

During the course of what seemed a very long night, my body grew hot and sweated profusely, soaking the sheets in what I assumed might be a fever caused by whatever was happening in my brain. I went through what seemed to be a long period of deep fear, suspecting that I had somehow damaged my nervous system. Yet, since that first night listening to the inner sounds, I have never experienced a headache or discomfort of any kind within my cranium.

Sometime in the early morning hours I fell asleep. When I awoke it was with great relief to find that my mind seemed to be back to normal, having returned to its familiar mode of verbalized thoughts, chatting away merrily once more. However, I now lived with these new memories and the realization that something singularly strange had occurred, something I had never been prepared for and that I had never previously encountered in books or in my life experience.

I continued to practice hatha yoga but spent increasingly long periods in silent meditation, finding that, now, I was able to fairly easily contact these resonant inner sounds. I began the practice of focusing on them while falling asleep and found that when I would begin to awaken from a dream in the middle of the night, I was able to quickly reenter the dream world by following these mysterious bright inner sounds.

My training in physics and electrical engineering led me to believe that these internal sounds were sine waves, not some sort of random noise. The tones also appeared to manifest in narrow spectrums centered about fundamental frequencies. For a time, I conjectured that they might be mechanical resonances within the physical structures of my inner ear. At work I began to experience, with great surprise, one of the high-pitched sounds flaring up in my cranium whenever I approached certain electronic equipment, computer screens, or even certain vending machines. At such moments I found myself internally verbalizing, with some humor, "Incoming!"—a phrase widely heard in the media at that time, from the front lines in Vietnam.

Over the next few weeks I noticed that during my meditation sessions, if I concentrated awareness within different physical/spatial locations within my body, such as the heart or the throat, perceptually different sounds would arise in different locations and patterns, though the sounds were most clear and pronounced in the central region of my brain.

I soon concluded that the source of these perceived inner sounds must be of an electromagnetic nature, possibly the vibrations of a neuronal plexus within my nervous system resonating with electro-magnetic modulations of our Earth's electromagnetic energy fields, or in the case of vending machines, the harmonic frequencies of some internal electrical radiation emanating from their circuitry, transform-ers, and so forth.

In bookstores, I began to browse through medical volumes describ-ing structures of the brain and the central nervous system. This was the age before the internet, but luckily I was living in New York City and had access not only to the New York Public Library but to many bookstores with medical sections. I was soon able to obtain excellent material with technical illustrations and X-ray photographs of internal physiological structures. I used these to visualize, with as much detail as possible, those internal areas, often corresponding with diagrams of the Indian chakra system, while meditating in the dark.

Over several years, this process of concentrating and visualizing within areas of my body while focusing on the sound tones as they would arise became a main source of meditative practice for me, and the inner sounds' tones grew ever more richly complex and often markedly louder in volume and began to produce distinct tactile sensations of a flowing nature, as if some warm inner current was beginning to stream within channels in my body.

On weekends I began to search for books detailing different techniques of meditation, and in the process discovered Patañjali's *Yoga Sūtra*. My first copy was a translation with commentaries by Professor Ernest E. Wood (1883–1965), having the rather impressive (and long) title of *Practical Yoga Ancient and Modern, Being a New, Independent Translation of Patañjali's Yoga Aphorisms, Interpreted in the Light of Ancient and Modern Psychological Knowledge and Practical Experience.*[8] I was thoroughly impressed that Wood had first been educated in the "hard" sciences of chemistry, physics, and geology, and only later had he become so thoroughly fascinated by yoga and meditation that he undertook to become a Sanskrit scholar. Wood's translations of the *Sūtra* seemed to me to be the perfect manual for the type of meditative exploration that had become my passion. After carefully studying Wood's translation for several months, I found a different translation of the *Yoga Sūtra* by a professor holding a Ph.D. in chemistry, I. K. Taimni (1898–1978).[9] To my surprise, many of the translations and commentaries differed markedly between the two books. This led me to attempt an understanding of each word in the context of my own experiences and practices.

As a direct consequence of the three major experiences that steered my interest from physics to metaphysics (i.e., the experience of LSD at night on the beach, the light in the forest at Hamilton Pool, and detection of the "inner sounds" in my New York apartment), I had discovered in the *Yoga Sūtra* what seemed to me to be an exceedingly useful, highly detailed, and integrated set of instructions and theory for psychonautic exploration through the means of prayer, meditation, and specific psychophysical exercises. More than simply a detailed handbook of "how to meditate," Patañjali's *Yoga Sūtra* presents a theory-practice continuum that includes, in the words of the scholar Ian Whicher, "effective definitions, explanations and descriptions of key concepts and terms relating to *theoria* and *praxis* in Yoga."[10]

Patañjali's *Yoga Sūtra* can be likened to a set of charts for navigation within the ocean of consciousness, much in the same way as the "rutters," written compilations of collected sailing experiences shared among Portuguese mariners, were used to cross oceans to new worlds prior to the development of scientifically calibrated nautical charts in the fourteenth and fifteenth centuries. The Portuguese rutters contained not only sketches, charts, and maps from firsthand accounts and direct observation but also a wealth of practical tips for exploring the New World oceans, pointing out such things as dangers to avoid, steering directions, and other practical instructions for those setting out on ocean voyages. In a similar fashion, Patañjali's *Sūtra* can be viewed as a collection of practical information, a rutter for those choosing to leave their egos anchored behind to set out for exploration on the vast oceans of consciousness. Patañjali's *Yoga Sūtra* is thus a compendium of integrated sailing instructions for the psychonaut. We are all immersed in various oceans of consciousness, but, like fish swimming in water, to us the waters of consciousness are invisible. And, when powerful, seemingly invisible currents of consciousness take hold and sweep us away to unfamiliar depths and strange regions of thought and sensation, disequilibrium may result.

Over the next few months I found additional English translations of the *Yoga Sūtra* in esoteric bookstores and soon had more than a dozen versions, each one expressing widely varied translations and interpretations of Patañjali's work. I soon realized that to develop my own understanding of this classic of contemplative yoga in the context of what I had been taught in physics, electronics, and communication theory, I would need to study Sanskrit in order to understand the various sūtras (or aphorisms) more precisely.

Influenced by my recent direct experiences of the numinous during prayer, meditation, and LSD, far outside of the domains of laboratory science, I found myself becoming something of a "black sheep" engineer, moving beyond a technical, materialist view of the world. My motivation was growing exponentially to understand consciousness in depth, academically *and* experientially, and to study the numinous with the conceptual tools of modern science. In my passion for studying these incredible new regions that were revealed to my inner eye, I soon dropped any previous career goals I might have had, replacing them with a concerted effort to explore these dimensions with the goal of mapping them in terms of physics and electronics.

For some time I wondered where I might find the means to study the Sanskrit language in New York. However, in 1973 the answer arrived during a three-day workshop on Asian traditions and contemplation, led by Alan Watts, a brilliant teacher of Asian studies who was visiting from California. During the introduction to the workshop, Alan mentioned that during the fall he would be teaching graduate academic classes in Asian philosophy at the California Institute of Asian Studies (CIAS) in San Francisco. He described the school as unique in that the teachers at CIAS were both academically as well as experientially qualified to teach in their respective subjects. I soon contacted the Institute and received a catalog, and to my amazement, not only were Sanskrit language courses part of the curriculum, but one of the teachers of Indian philosophy at the school was Rammurti Mishra, the author of a 538-page treatise on what I considered to be one of the most detailed translations of the *Yoga Sūtra*.[11]

I soon applied for admission to the California Institute of Asian Studies, though with some trepidation, concerned that my academic background in physics and engineering might not meet with approval for acceptance into an academic philosophy department. However, to my delight I received a formal letter of admission, and the following spring, having worked for five years as an electrical engineer in New York, I found myself traveling to San Francisco to enroll in a program of comparative Asian philosophy and religion. Finally, I was able to study Sanskrit and Indian philosophy in a formal setting. Three years later I completed my M.A. program in Indian philosophy, successfully publishing my thesis, "The History, Philosophy, and Practice of Tantra in South India." Shortly thereafter I married a Buddhist classmate from CIAS, and over the next two years had a son and daughter in succession. Then, we all moved to the east coast of Saudi Arabia to work for ARAMCO, a large oil company, for the next nineteen years. Living in the Arabian desert afforded me much quiet time (early in the morning) to continue my practice of silent contemplation.

AYAHUASCA AND THE PSYCHIC NANOBOTS

When I came back to San Francisco after the long sojourn in Saudi Arabia, I returned to the Institute, which by then had changed its name to the California Institute of Integral Studies, and I entered a doctoral program in philosophy, cosmology, and consciousness to study under Brian Swimme and Robert McDermott. After several decades without using entheogens other than cannabis, decades in which my contemplative practice had grown substantially in regularity and richer in experience, I was soon afforded the opportunity to participate in a small group working with a shaman from Ecuador to explore the use of the plant ayahuasca in a "healing meditation." The session was held at night with a dozen other participants in a large room in the middle of a redwood forest.

After about an hour and a half I suddenly noticed that a large fan hanging from the ceiling above was writhing, and as I looked up I saw that what had been blades were now a huge black snake, writhing. At that point I had to urinate very intensely and got up to move toward the bathroom, but when I looked down I saw the floor covered with a sea of smaller writhing black snakes. I stepped on one and slipped backward. The next thing I recall is lying down on my back with the shaman fanning me with several large tobacco leaves and blowing tobacco over my face, after which I was able to stand up.

After returning from the bathroom I found a place to lie down and closed my eyes. Many things were felt and, it seemed, several "stages" passed through, and I will relate only the most intense experience that I have been able to recall. At some point I felt that I was literally being taken apart. In fact, I was being so thoroughly analyzed, tested, tasted, and probed that I had a sudden fear that I might lose my "personality" or ego—that I would never be able to be the person I thought I was again. I felt as if I were being subjected to cosmic plasma-magnetic entity rape, and for a brief time felt outrage, fear, and panic, but that quickly passed. (Much of the time during the ayahuasca experience I found my years of practicing various mantras in Latin, Sanskrit, and English helped immensely, as I was able to fall back to focusing on a mantra in a specific location of the body-mind as if it were an old friend.)

The outrage passed as I felt the "invasion" to be of a benign character having almost a caring quality. I was not being violated after all; instead, I was being "tuned" somehow at a very fundamental level, at what seemed to be a molecular, organic level or perhaps even lower, at a genetic or electronic level. At about that time I became significantly calmer as I began to sense the effects of the benevolent "tuning." I suddenly realized what people mean when they say the plants are "medicine," although I've always been exceptionally blessed with health and seldom needed healing in the ordinary sense. But this healing or tuning had a different, deeper, psycho-physical or neuro-physical sense to it. It was a healing of "being."

Visually, what I was observing during that time was stunning. I was floating somewhere off to the side of an enormous slab rising up from below and continuing upward to pass far beyond my perception, appearing like some behemoth intergalactic construct from a *Battlestar Galactica* or *Star Wars* set. It consisted of a myriad of complex, interlocking, angular shapes, components that continued to dissolve and reform like hyperactive transformer-robot assemblies, constantly changing as if self-modifying resonantly in synch with my own interactive experience of observation and being observed.

I was floating alongside the slab from what seemed to be thirty feet away, viewing the phenomenon as a bird might view an enormous skyscraper. From time to time a separate wire-frame entity would detach from the slab and slowly float in my direction, only to suddenly accelerate in a different trajectory to move behind me, beyond my range of vision. For some reason the words *psychic nanobots* arose in my mind.

To my amazement, these nanobots were responding to my own presence, and indeed they seemed to be the source of the "probe" and "tuning" that was simultaneously going on so intimately within my own body that I had initially felt that I was being unwillingly violated. This probing went on for what felt like a very long time, during the latter part of which I found myself completely calm, receptive, and surprisingly grateful. In fact, I felt in some way that I was trading with these plasma-magnetic entities or electrobiological nanobots; they were imparting to me a vibratory "tune up" while receiving something in return, though what I could not say.

For a long time it felt as if these psychic (or spiritual) nanobots were performing a kind of vehicle recall analysis or 100,000-mile checkup: tuning my many energy dimensions, physical and psychophysical systems, and prescribing and applying immediately the compensatory radiation-resonance tweaking treatments required in my resonating energy systems, perhaps at the quantum level, the DNA level, the molecular level, the cellular level, the neuronal level, the electromagnetic plasmic level, and other as yet unknown "levels" of being. Six hours later, however, to my surprise—and all of the next day and the following week—my senses of well-being, alertness, and joy were all enhanced, amplified, and seemed to be operating at higher levels than normal.

This experience afforded me a new respect for the characterization of ayahuasca and other "healing plants" through their imparting to me a new understanding of the meaning of the concept of healing, which now implies a new urgency—a healing not only of me as an individual but of the entire ecology, the planet. I think something the vine energy-nanobot-plasma-magnetic entities did for me was strengthen what had been weak or broken links with the ecosphere. After that night, I felt an even greater concern for the planet and the animals and plants around me, and I was charged with a new enthusiasm for my efforts to understand consciousness in all its mysterious ramifications.

While such intense experiences, powered by entheogens, can both motivate and inspire us to explore the mysterious depths of consciousness, what is of equal value are the written legacies of others who have sailed these rarified regions. In previous chapters we have primarily considered guidance left by two such explorers, Steiner and Patañjali. We now turn to Patañjali's home, the Indian subcontinent, where we will find an even wider range of approaches developed over the millennia by Indian psychonauts that reveal a wide range of time-tested techniques for the development and awakening of these new organs of perception. These directions are often couched in the symbolic language of Tantra.

6

Indian Tantra and
Supersensible Perception

While Steiner's voluminous discussions about the significance of and major approaches to supersensible perception are clear, it is to the Indian subcontinent that we must turn for explicit techniques and exercises for the successful awakening and development of these new organs of perception. These directions are often couched in the symbolic language of Tantra.

Over the past millennia Indian sages and mystics, using direct participatory experimental methods to accomplish what we might call psychophysical research, recorded and handed down their experimental discoveries and instructional techniques for attaining specific supersensible states of perception. Their findings and polished techniques are to be found in the encoded cultural trappings of what is generally known as Tantra Shastra (scripture, teaching, or rules) in traditional southern India. Ironically, just the mention of the word *tantra* in the West has ranged historically from outrage to condemnation, beginning with British culture in the eighteenth century confronting the highly pornographic (to the Victorians) Indian temple carvings in their myriad of beautifully carved (Tantric) poses, and continuing—though increasingly less frequently as America's sense of morality evolves—among contemporary conservatives who disparage weekend Tantric sex workshops held in the California countryside by post–New Agers.

But a broader and more accurate understanding of Tantra lies in the extraordinarily precise detail with which the texts describe interior transformations of conscious energy, along with numerous techniques for modulating and transforming the consciousness of the perceiver. It is from these re-creatable Tantric methodologies and models explaining the dynamics of conscious energy that there emerges a possible coherency upon which to develop a new psychophysical view of consciousness itself, a new psychophysics.

In this chapter we will explain elements of the major exercises described by the Sanskrit terms *mantra, yantra, chakra, samādhi,* and *kuṇḍalinī.*

MANTRA AND AUDITORY RESONANCE

Mantra can be seen as much more than words, even sacred words, though all prayer can be mantra. Even single words or sounds, repeated over and over, are mantra when practiced with as continuous a focus of awareness as possible. Of course, the mantra—the repetition—does not have to be audible; it can be a silent repetition, which is internally audible. The audible resonance is consciousness itself, and internal repetition leads to contact with the source of the vibrations in the frequency domain of consciousness, allowing supersensuous perception to arise.

> Mantra are considered, not products of discursive thought, human wisdom or poetic phantasy, but flash-lights of the eternal truth, seen by those eminent men who have come into a supersensuous contact with the Unseen.[1]

As the scientist and Indian philosopher I. K. Taimni (who obtained his Ph.D. in inorganic chemistry from London University in 1928 and later became the president of the Theosophical Society in Adyar) writes:

> The aim of all mantra, in short, is to purify and harmonise the vehicles of the seeker so that they become increasingly sensitive to the subtler layers of his own spiritual consciousness. As he comes into contact with these he becomes increasingly aware of that Reality of which his own consciousness is a partial expression.[2]

Rephrasing this statement in psychophysical terms, we would say that the aim of mantra is to tune into or to resonate with a particular bandwidth of energy frequencies, a spectrum of energy accessible to our own consciousness that can be contacted through mantric vibration resonating in a bandwidth of atemporal conscious energy.

Within this bandwidth or region of consciousness (which cannot even really be called a region as it is both nontemporal and nonspatial, outside of time and space), in what is called the frequency domain in the EMF field theory of consciousness, can be found all of the vibrations that have ever been generated, interpenetrating in all of their complexities. In many Indian schools of thought this is called the *ākāśa,* or *alaya-vijñāna,* the "storehouse of all consciousness," and it is this domain that is "touched" by the contemplative Tantric yogi during sessions reaching *asamprajñata samādhi,* when the various separate cognitive systems of thought and perception have been attenuated and the deepest silence has been entered.

It is ironic that in order to reach this state of asamprajñāta samādhi and touch the Akashic records, even short-term and long-term memory must be "silenced," detached, attenuated, or deactivated. Hence the difficulty (back in the world of time and space) of communicating the "experience" or of describing this state, and thus the resulting myriad metaphors and symbols throughout cultures and religions serving as substitutes for the authentic experience that is so difficult to recall.

YANTRA AND VISUAL RESONANCE

I bow to the Goddess who is the Soul of all Yantras.
LALITĀSAHASRANĀMA

The Sanskrit word *yantra* derives etymologically from the root *yam,* which is translated as "to sustain," "hold" or "support." In common usage it can be used to refer to any physical structure that may be used to support exercises for the health, growth, and evolutionary transformation of consciousness. The scholar Madhu Khanna characterizes yantras as "aids to and the chief instruments of meditative discipline . . . a yantra used in this context and for this purpose is an abstract geometrical design intended as a 'tool' for meditation and increased awareness."[3]

Among yantras, the Sri Yantra is highly revered as an advanced contemplative instrument. Figure 6.1 on page 76 shows the image of a Sri Yantra created by the author out of wood, gold, and ground mineral pigments tempered in egg yolk. The mantra of the yantra (which resonates with the yantra when recited and invokes the energy deities associated with the yantra) can be seen in Devanagari script in a circle just within the inner surrounding row of petals in the yantra. In this instance, the mantra consists of single "seed syllables," basic unique sound patterns that the contemplative associates with various chakra locations within the body. While reciting each syllable (audibly or inaudibly), the practitioner also focuses awareness spatially within the general area of the syllable's corresponding chakra location within the body. For example, while repeating the first syllable of most such mantras, *Om*, the practitioner focuses on the center of the head or cranial cavity, trying to feel a sensation in the region close to the hypothalamus and pineal gland.

The yantra is also used as a mnemonic tool, which helps the practitioner recall a variety of attributes and issues that should be made consciously explicit in the psychophysical practices leading to the transformative experiential dimensions associated with the yantra.

For example, in the image of the Sri Yantra shown in figure 6.2 on page 76, the outer linear shape conveys the idea of fortress walls facing in the four cardinal directions. In order for the contemplative to move psychophysically toward the center of the yantra (the central dot is called the *bindu*), all of these external attributes must be dealt with and harmonized in the life of the practitioner. Generally, what exists outside the gates of the yantra is what we experience of the world through sense activity and cravings of our ego constructs. Before gaining entrance to richer psychophysical experience, the one who begins to use the yantra must work on dealing with and transforming such things as worldly desire, anger, avarice and greed, infatuation, obstinacy, hubris, jealousy, and desire for earthly rewards and self-recognition. In order for all of

Fig. 6.1. Author's Sri Yantra. Tempera and gold on wood.

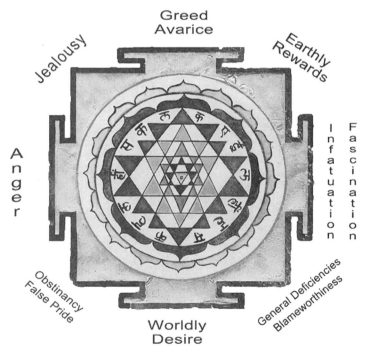

Fig. 6.2. Author's Sri Yantra, mapped for contemplation.

these issues to be systematically approached and focused on during the beginning of each meditation period, the yantra associates these issues with specific parts of the surrounding shape of the yantra.

CHAKRA: LOCUS OF PHYSIOLOGICAL RESONANCE

Contemplatives have discovered loci within the human physiology that are particularly sensitive and resonate when one's focus of consciousness can be maintained within a region for an extended period of time. These locations are designated by the Sanskrit term *chakra*. The contemplative sage M. P. Pandit, a follower of Sri Aurobindo and resident of Pondicherry in southern India, has written extensively on chakras.

> There are in the being of man certain nodii which are so to say centres connecting him with other universal planes of existence; and when properly tapped they open up in one's being their respective planes and the powers that are characteristic of the principles governing those planes. Within the Indian Yogic system, these are called "chakras" or "Centers."[4]

A more Western, medicalized description of these areas was presented in 1926 before the Bombay Medical Union by Dr. Vasant Rele, who read a paper for those interested in "the science of Yoga." Rele presented a theoretical psychophysical explanation for some of the experiential changes in consciousness described by yogis as a result of Tantric practices, and in particular, the activation of the kuṇḍalinī, the "Serpent Power." Rele also happened to be a close friend and associate of the chief justice of the Supreme Court in India (1915), Sir John Woodroffe, known also by his pen name "Sir Arthur Avalon," a pseudonym with which he himself had published numerous books about, and translations of, Tantric material.

The chakra is experienced as a psychophysical matrix with a definite spatial location within the human body. Diagrams of chakras are used as maps for locating regions within which to focus consciousness during meditation. Major chakras appear as blossoming energy at the fontanelle, forehead, throat, heart, navel, and coccyx (fig. 6.3). Dr. Vasant Rele describes the ājñā chakra, for example, at the level of the forehead:

> This *chakra* is the naso-ciliary extension of the cavernous plexus of the sympathetic through the ophthalmic division of the fifth cranial

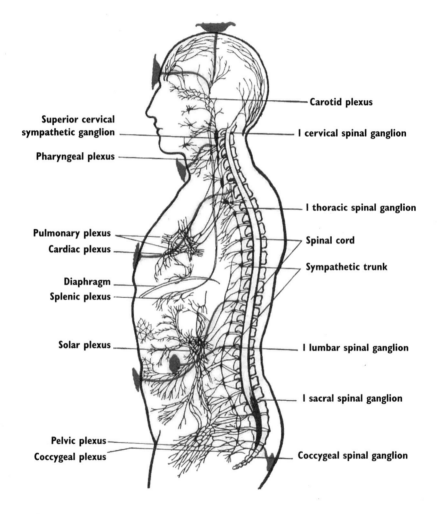

Fig. 6.3. Chakra diagram relative to nervous plexuses.
C. W. Leadbeater first published the idea of the chakras for the West
in The Chakras, *1927.*

nerve, ending in the ciliary muscles of the iris and at the root of the nose, through the supra-orbital foramen. It has two petals or branches and is situated between the eye-brows. It is the spot which is contemplated while undergoing the process of *prāṇāyāma*.[5]

A map of multiple chakra locations that have been identified by contemplatives can be seen in a Nepalese *thangka* from the sixteenth century, most likely painted by a Tibetan monk (fig. 6.4).

Fig. 6.4. Chakra figure diagram.
Author's Nepalese thangka, sixteenth century CE.

SAMĀDHI: PSYCHOPHYSICAL TUNING
OF HUMAN CONSCIOUSNESS

In the *Yoga Sūtra,* Patañjali tells us that the ultimate goal of yoga is "the union of the individual self (*jīvātman*) with the transcendent Self (*paramātman*)."[6] In the *Yoga Sūtra* we find an elaborate map of human consciousness with explicit methods for traveling among the various regions described in that map. In the 195 aphorisms that compose the *Yoga Sūtra* as gathered together by Patañjali are revealed the collective experiential wisdom distilled over the lifetimes of generations of Indian sages, aphorisms that have been compiled with a stamp of authenticity. That there is a great deal of real, enduring, and practical validity to Patañjali's map can be inferred by the many translations and written commentaries that have sprung up, beginning as early as the seventh century with Vyāsa's work.

In a series of terse sūtras (mnemonic threads, from the root *siv,* "to sew," the root of our medical word *suture*), Patañjali constructs a pragmatic model for human access to states of awareness rarely found in human experience. The descriptions of these states and dimensions of consciousness, and the instruction given for navigating among them, are the outgrowth of direct observation contributed from age to age through a long lineage of contemplative seekers in India; they are obviously of significant interest to Patañjali.

The word *yoga* is often translated as "yoke," "to link," or "to unite."[7] The word *yoga* is understood numerous ways in the West, typically as a form of exercise consisting of extreme body-stretching poses. But a contemporary yoga scholar says that when the word "is used by itself without any qualification, it refers to the path of meditation, particularly as outlined in the *Yoga Sūtras*—the Aphorisms on Yoga—and the term *yogi,* a practitioner of this type of meditational yoga."[8]

But the word *yoga* is also synonymous with *samādhi* in the *Yoga Sūtra.* The importance of attaining the state of samādhi lies in the ensuing ability to discover numerous ways of controlling, redirecting, and modifying mental activities to establish transcendent* links, unions, and communions with alternate states of conscious awareness.

Dhāraṇā

The third chapter of the *Yoga Sūtra* assumes that the material in the two previous chapters has been mastered, and in that third chapter Patañjali focuses at the outset on the three specific instructions for entering into samādhi. This is followed by an enumeration of various powers that may be experienced.

Here again, the first sūtra of chapter 3 is the most important, describing the first of two primary skills required to be developed and exercised in order to discover how to shift consciousness into the state of samādhi. Patañjali defines the first skill, *dhāraṇā* ("concentration"), as the practice of holding the "stuff" of consciousness steadily within one place, one locus within a fixed region of the human body or on a fixed concept such as a Zen koan, a short repeated string of sounds (mantra), or a visual image (e.g., a Tibetan thangka, a Russian orthodox icon, or a candle flame).

Sūtra III.1

Deśa-bandhaś cittasya dhāraṇā

Focusing citta consciousness within a specific place is called dhāraṇā.[9]

देशबन्धश्चित्तस्य धारणा ।

Fig. 6.5. Yoga Sūtra III.1 in Devanagari script.

Dhāraṇā is the initial skill that must be developed in the practice of contemplation. Without realizing that they have developed the skill,

---

*The term *transcendent* as used in this book is to be contrasted with "ordinary every-day waking" consciousness; the transcendent is a state or condition of awareness beyond verbal-emotional ego boundaries, one that is numinous, sublime, and inexpressible, as elaborated by Patañjali in his descriptive injunctions defining the various stages and states of samādhi and kaivalya ("completeness through integration," or absolute release).

many students in modern educational systems have already mastered the basic technique of dhāraṇā to some degree. It is the skill of being able to concentrate one's conscious awareness in one place (*deśa*), the more focused the better. Accordingly, one would think that adepts at electronic gaming might have this skill in a highly developed form. However, it is not enough to be able to gather consciousness to focus within a bounded area momentarily. What is required is to focus awareness within a specific, limited region (spatial, auditory, or visual) and *to hold this focus steadily* within the region chosen for a sustained period of time while other operations of the brain-mind remain suspended.

Dhyāna

Dhyāna is the second skill that must be developed on the path to the acquisition of supersensible perception (i.e., the state of awareness that Patañjali calls samādhi). Mastery of dhyāna leads directly to samādhi. The technique or state of dhyāna is that of "holding" one's focus steadily without being diverted by distractions, and more importantly, to develop the capability *to sustain this focus unwaveringly* for a protracted period of time. Patañjali defines the term *dhyāna* in the following sūtra.

Sūtra III.2

Tatra pratyaya-ekatānatā dhyānam

*Here the content of awareness held in a single stream
is called dhyāna.*[10]

तत्र प्रत्ययैकतानता ध्यानम्

Fig. 6.6. Yoga Sūtra III.2 in Devanagari script.

The word *dhyāna* has been translated into Chinese as Chán (禪) and into Japanese as Zen. The focus of the sequence dhāraṇā dhyāna can be varied: a mantra (voiced or internally audible sutra or prayer), a yantra (usually a visual, painted diagram), a concept, or an inner sensation, and so on. In advanced practice the object is actually not an object at all, and the adept learns to focus on "consciousness-without-an-object," a sort of void of objects.

The key here is to be able to sustain this bounded focus of consciousness within such a particular region for a sufficient length of time with an intensity of focus so as to ignite transition into the state called samādhi, the subject of the next sūtra. An analogy might be seen in using a magnifying glass lens to focus the rays of the sun on an object in order to ignite the object into flame. In focusing with the glass lens, the object is usually a leaf or a twig, whereas in focusing consciousness the object is a repeated prayer (mantra), image (yantra), concept (such as love, death, detachment), external point (candle flame, cloud), or internal bodily location or sensation.

Samādhi

Success in this dhāraṇā dhyāna sequence is obtained with a shift or threshold crossing of consciousness into a state of samādhi, an event that the great philosopher of religion Mircea Eliade, in describing the "ascent to heaven" or the mystical flight of the shaman, has termed the "rupture of plane."[11] Patañjali describes the acquisition of this state with the term *samādhi,* which he defines here in the third sūtra.

Sūtra III.3

Tadeva-artha-mātra-nirbhāsaṁ
svarūpa-śūnyam-iva-samādhiḥ

Samādhi is when that same dhyāna shines forth as the object alone and [the mind] is devoid of its own [reflective] nature.[12]

$$\text{तदेवार्थमात्रनिर्भासं स्वरूपशून्यमिव समाधिः ।}$$

Fig. 6.7. Yoga Sūtra III.3.

The rest of the third chapter describes numerous siddhis or "powers" that have been found by contemplatives when exploring the domains of consciousness opened up through entry into supersensible perception within the oceanic realm of radiant *puruṣa* ("self of pure consciousness")[13] through achieving the state of samādhi. These siddhis include such things as communication with other centers of consciousness, communion with the dead, remote sensing, perception of inner sound vibrations, and viewing phosphorescent visual images.

KUṆḌALINĪ POWER: CIRCULATION OF LIGHT

One of the earliest published scientific accounts of the kuṇḍalinī was written by Dr. Vasant Rele in 1927. Based on a series of lectures he gave on the topic, Rele's book was called *The Mysterious Kundalini: The Physical Basis of the "Kundalini Yoga."*[14] Rele asserts that the kuṇḍalinī corresponds to energy flowing in the right vagus nerve. He says that a yogi, through the vagus nerve, "establishes a complete control over the unconscious automatic action of the involuntary muscular fibres."[15] This accords well with the *Hatha-Yoga-Pradipika,* in which the kuṇḍalinī is said "to be lying dormant guarding the opening of the passage that leads to the seat of Brahma." Rele goes on to describe the very physiological substrate of yogic processes when he says:

> This seat is said to be *Brahma-randhra* (cave of Brahma), that is, the ventricular cavity in the brain. . . . Unless she (*Kundalini*) is awakened, or made consciously active, one cannot send one's embodied soul (*Jivātma*), which is supposed to reside in the heart (*Hridaya*), along the *Sushumnā nādi* to the *Brahma-randhra* nor is he able to assist the soul captured in the *Randhra,* to be freed to join the Universal Soul (*Paramātmā*) outside.[16]

Here Rele is careful to explain that his understanding of the English translation of the Sanskrit word *randhra* is definitely "cavity" and should not be translated as "hole," as is found in numerous other English translations. He states that this randhra is "the inter-communicating cavity of the four ventricles of the brain and is continuous with the central canal (*Chitra*) of the spinal cord (*Sushumnā nādi*)."[17] A physiologically

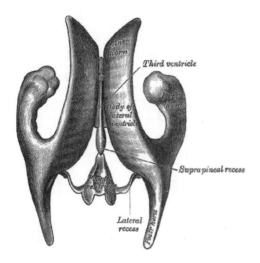

Fig. 6.8. Sketch of ventricular cavities, viewed from above and to the rear. First published in Henry Gray, Anatomy of the Human Body, *1918.*

accurate sketch of the ventricular cavities within the brain can be seen in figure 6.8, viewed from above and to the rear.

Thus the experience of the movement or flow of kuṇḍalinī energy might also be seen or understood as the phenomenon of a magnetic plasma field being tuned to a resonant frequency within the ventricular "Cave of Brahma."

Microwave cavities, also known as electromagnetic cavity radiators, are to the invisible-frequency energy spectrum what lenses are to visible light energy. During my senior year of electrical engineering, we were given the project of designing resonant waveguide cavity horn antennas for amplification and modulation of microwave energy fields.

In a course on the electrophysiology of the nervous system, I noticed the striking similarities between the waveguide horn antennas we were designing in the communication lab and the images of the ventricular cavities within the human skull. I mentioned this in class and was told by my professor that the ventricular system seemed to exist only to cushion shock trauma to the brain and perhaps to help equalize temperature.

If human physiology does indeed incorporate an electromagnetic-frequency energy component, then the horn-shaped ventricular cavities within the cranial cavity indicate the possibility that nature might very well have already designed and implemented its own energy-frequency signal communication system.

7

The Cosmology of Consciousness

What does modern science say about consciousness and the possibility of supersensible perception as described by Rudolf Steiner and Patañjali? Contemporary maps of consciousness drawn up by physicists and biologists say nothing about supersensible perception. Yet, as our inner eye becomes sensitized to completely new regions of consciousness, we may soon find ourselves lost in vast unfamiliar territories. It is possible that we may become confused, overwhelmed, or even frightened unless we have some kind of map to fall back on. Accordingly, readers are encouraged to make every effort here to grasp the fundamentals of "how consciousness works." The maps of consciousness presented in this chapter (a cosmological map) and the next (a physiological map) will be invaluable for those first encountering the threshold of supersensible regions.

BASIC QUANTUM PHYSICS
AND THE LIMITS OF SPACE

An understanding of the basic concepts of quantum physics begins with its father, Max Planck (1858–1947), whose pioneering paper in 1900 gave birth to what is now known as quantum theory. Planck came from an intellectual family in Prussia, where both his grandfather and great-grandfather had been professors of theology. In his early years, Planck was drawn to music and not only learned to play the piano, organ, and cello but also composed music, including an opera. Nevertheless, his attraction to science led to an early passion for physics and an eventual Ph.D. in the abstract field of thermodynamics. The following newspaper account of a 1931 interview with the seventy-three-year-old Planck reveals a fascinating observation on the role of consciousness in the universe that will likely surprise many modern physicists:

> **INTERVIEWER:** "Do you think that consciousness can be explained in terms of matter and its laws?"

> **MAX PLANCK:** "No. I regard consciousness as fundamental. I regard matter as derivative from consciousness. We cannot get behind consciousness. Everything that we talk about, everything that we regard as existing, postulates consciousness."[1]

Later, the interviewer commented on Planck's demeanor:

> In my interview with him, Professor Planck replied to all my questions with a quite remarkable lack of hesitation. It would seem that his ideas on these subjects are now definitely formed, or else that he thinks with remarkable rapidity—probably both suppositions are true.[2]

In his 1900 paper, Planck used fundamental constants of the universe, including the speed of light and the gravitational constant, to calculate the value of two cosmic constants that his colleagues later called "Planck constants."

Planck length: 1.616199×10^{-35} meter

Planck time constant: 5.39106×10^{-44} second

The Planck length is constrained by the speed of light. Here is a simple check:

Visualize an incident photon, a single quantum of light energy as it speeds in from the left, moving toward the right edge of the page.

Assume that the photon traverses the distance of one Planck length. What is its velocity? (Hint: divide distance by time.) Dividing the

Planck Length (ℓ_P) and Planck Time (t_P)

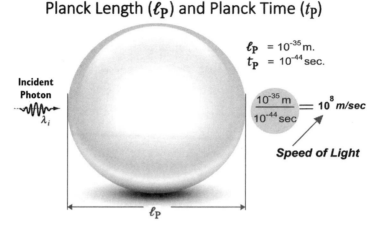

$\ell_P = 10^{-35}$ m.
$t_P = 10^{-44}$ sec.

Incident
Photon
λ_i

$$\frac{10^{-35}\,\text{m}}{10^{-44}\,\text{sec}} = 10^8\ m/sec$$

Speed of Light

ℓ_P

Fig. 7.1. The two quantum constants:
Planck length and Planck time.

distance traversed by the time required yields 2.99792458×10^8 meters/ second, the speed of light (fig. 7.1).

The Planck length and the Planck time constants are the very fundamental granular measurements of space and time in the universe. Because of the proven invariance of the speed of light, nothing below the Planck length can exist in space, nor can there be any time interval smaller than the Planck time constant. Everything in space-time begins, at the bottom of the universe, from these two constant values. Nothing can be smaller in time or space. This basic discovery of quantum mechanics has led directly to the laser, the atom bomb, and the iPhone.

But if neither space nor time can exist below the surface of a Planck-diameter spherical boundary, what *does* exist within that sphere? The astounding answer, according to the conclusion arrived at by the neuro-physicist Karl Pribram and the quantum physicist David Bohm, is that within this mysterious region that has no space nor time is *consciousness itself*. As we shall soon discover, a deeper understanding of this quantum model of consciousness will be the key to unlock supersensible perception.

In his cosmology, Bohm visualized the universe as consisting of two separate yet interpenetrating regions that he called the *explicate order* and the *implicate order*. According to Bohm, that which begins where space ends, beneath the boundary of the Planck-diameter sphere as illustrated in figure 7.1, is the region known as the implicate order. Bohm's theory describes a quantum process by which the explicate order, our familiar space-time universe, unfolds *out from within* its true source in the implicate order. But this is a two-way process: everything that subsequently occurs in our universe of space and time generates informed energy (information) that continuously folds back into the implicate order. In this process information is never truly lost, but continuously and eternally recycles between the explicate order and the implicate order. According to Bohm and Pribram it is this mysterious inner region, the spaceless, timeless region of the implicate order, that not only is the primary source of conscious awareness, but that also functions as the storage repository of collective memory. This cosmology of consciousness developed by Pribram and Bohm has come to be known as the Pribram-Bohm holoflux theory of consciousness.

The technical basics of the holoflux theory of consciousness can be summarized in three assertions.

1. Consciousness exists everywhere as an information-encoded energy field.
2. The universe consists of two distinct regions or domains: the explicate order (that which we know as space-time) and the implicate order (a transcendent domain outside of space-time).
3. Consciousness in the explicate order manifests as *electromagnetic* energy, interacting with consciousness in the implicate order that manifests there as *holoflux* energy.

Both the explicate order (our daily experience) and the implicate order exist as realities. However, the implicate region is located at extremely small dimensions, where space ends, below the size of the Planck length boundary of 10^{-35} meter. Supersensible experience in the implicate order is transcendent, outside of space-time.

To better understand the topology of the implicate order and the

Planck length, a thought experiment is useful here. In your mind's eye, imagine a sphere about the size of a grain of sand or a pixel, and assume that it has even smaller dimensions within, that it has an "inside."

Now we begin moving radially, inward, geometrically, toward the center. Imagine that as we move inward toward the center, we are also shrinking in scale, becoming smaller and smaller as we continue on our journey. We eventually find ourselves at 10^{-15} meter, the diameter of a proton of a hydrogen atom. Shrinking another tenfold we arrive at 10^{-16} meter, the size of an electron. Eventually, we reach a radius of 10^{-17} meter, the size of a Higgs Boson. We are now as deep as contemporary measurements have been able to go, at the limit of the Large Hadron Collider. But let us continue moving inward, shrinking toward the geometric center until we reach the very bottom limit of space, the Planck length of 10^{-35} meter. This is the end of the line. We have reached the bottom limit of space . . . or have we? Bohm doesn't think so, and I quote from his book *Wholeness and the Implicate Order*:

> To suppose that there is nothing *beyond* this limit at all would indeed be quite arbitrary. Rather, it is very probable that beyond it lies a further domain, or set of domains, of the nature of which we have as yet little or no idea.[3]

The Pribram-Bohm hypothesis holds that there are definite limits to the dimensions of space and time. Physicists tell us that there exist additional dimensions beyond space and time, yet we do not normally perceive such dimensions. According to Bernard Carr, professor of mathematics and astronomy at the University of London:

> The Universe may have more than the three dimensions of space that we actually observe, with the extra dimensions being compactified on the Planck scale (the distance of 10^{-35} meters, at which quantum gravity effects become important), so that we do not notice them. . . . In particular, physics has revealed a unity about the Universe which makes it clear that everything is connected in a way which

would have seemed inconceivable a few decades ago. The discovery of dark dimensions through particle physics shakes our view of the nature of reality just as profoundly as the discovery of dark energy through cosmology.[4]

Carr uses the alchemical image of the ouroboros (fig. 7.2) to illustrate his GUT (grand unified theory) in describing the full but limited range of the physical world in space. He says, "The significance of the head meeting the tail is that the entire Universe was once compressed to a point of infinite density (or, more strictly, the Planck density)."[5] This archetypal figure implies the interconnectedness of the entire universal process in time and space, presenting a cybernetic feedback loop operational at every scale. Mystics have intuited this ouroboric process symbolized in the images of a snake swallowing its own tail (the image has been found as early as the fourteenth century BCE in the tomb of Tutankhamen), and it is frequently used to symbolize cybernetic feedback in control-and-communication theory.[6] While Norbert Wiener coined the term *cybernetics*, communication engineers would more commonly see this as a metaphor for the "feedback loop," used everywhere in electronic circuit design.

Stretching out this circular cosmic serpent from head to tail, one can create an axis of scales that encompasses all of space. In figure 7.3,

Fig. 7.2. Alchemical ouroboros (ca. 1478 by unknown illustrator). First published 1478, Codex Parisinus graecus 2327, *fol. 279.*

such a scale is drawn starting with the currently estimated diameter of the universe itself at 10^{+25} meters, and descending down to the Planck length boundary at 10^{-35} of a meter. The axis thus spans a total range of 10^{+60} meters (60 jumps by the power of 10). The Pribram-Bohm hypothesis holds that there, at the very bottom of the linear scale, is to be found the transition between the explicate order and the implicate order.[7] Here, at the bottom limit, space reaches its *end,* according to

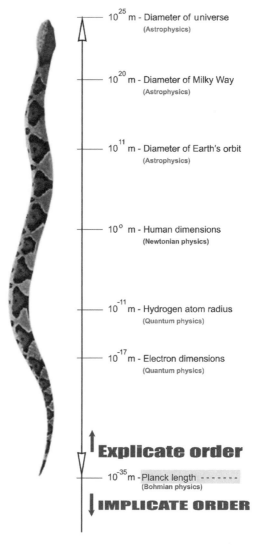

10^{25} m - Diameter of universe
(Astrophysics)

10^{20} m - Diameter of Milky Way
(Astrophysics)

10^{11} m - Diameter of Earth's orbit
(Astrophysics)

10^{0} m - Human dimensions
(Newtonian physics)

10^{-11} m - Hydrogen atom radius
(Quantum physics)

10^{-17} m - Electron dimensions
(Quantum physics)

Explicate order

10^{-35} m - Planck length -------
(Bohmian physics)

IMPLICATE ORDER

Fig. 7.3. Scales of dimensional space and the explicate/implicate boundary.

modern physics—but it also marks the *entry point* into Bohm's "implicate order," the same region that Pribram and Fourier term the "frequency domain."[8]

The implications of this are profound. Imagine moving inward, shrinking in size, ever closer toward the center, and abruptly finding that you can go no further, that you have reached the bottom limit of space. You find that this is not a flat sea bottom, but appears as if you are standing on the surface of a sphere or globe, the tiniest one possible, a sphere with an inner diameter of only 10^{-35} meter, the Planck length limit to space. Below you space does not exist.

Here the boundary has been reached between space and the transcendental infinity of the implicate order; this is the event horizon, a boundary zone between space and the implicate order. To understand this, one must realize that the classical Cartesian assumption that space is linear and continuous is *wrong;* there *is* indeed a bottom to space, at least according to physics, below which space no longer has meaning. It is here that we have located the fundamental and inescapable quantum discontinuity, as David Bohm and F. David Peat describe the granularity of space:

> What of the order between two points in space? The Cartesian order holds that space is continuous. Between any two points, no matter how close they lie, occur an infinite of other points. Between any two neighboring points in this infinity lies another infinity and so on. This notion of continuity is not compatible with the order of quantum theory. . . . The physicist John Wheeler has suggested that, at very short distances, continuous space begins to break up into a foam-like structure. Thus the "order between" two points moves from the order of continuity to an order of a discontinuous foam.[9]

THE "HARD PROBLEM" OF DAVID CHALMERS

Perhaps the most widely debated issue in consciousness studies can be found encapsulated in the phrase "the hard problem of consciousness," first coined by David Chalmers in a 1995 essay in which he places emphasis squarely on the issue of *experience*. Chalmers proposes a theory of consciousness that highlights the importance of information, but it is the *experience* of information that he calls the "hard problem."

> The really hard problem of consciousness is the problem of *experience*. When we think and perceive, there is a whir of information processing, but there is also a subjective aspect. . . . Why should physical processing give rise to a rich inner life at all? It seems objectively unreasonable that it should, and yet it does. If any problem qualifies as *the* problem of consciousness, it is this one.[10]

This "whir of information processing" Chalmers refers to is readily observed in the electrical information processing of the neuronal brain system in the body, like the "thinking meat" that so astounded two alien observers in a story by the science fiction writer Terry Bisson.

> "They're meat all the way through."
>
> "No brain?"
>
> "Oh, there is a brain all right. It's just that the brain is made out of meat!"
>
> "So . . . what does the thinking?"
>
> "You're not understanding, are you? . . . The brain does the thinking. The meat."
>
> "Thinking meat! You're asking me to believe in thinking meat!"
>
> "Yes, thinking meat! Conscious meat! Loving meat. Dreaming meat. The meat is the whole deal! Are you beginning to get the picture?"
>
> "Omigod. You're serious then. They're made out of meat."[11]

The data stored and manipulated within modern electronic technologies is a property of physical processes and only becomes information when presented to the conscious perception of a human reader. Within the computational space of the computer itself, the information is merely symbolic code, assumed physically to be unconscious. Chalmers posits a theory of consciousness that is the union of experience and the physical.

> A non-reductive theory of consciousness will consist in a number of *psychophysical principles*, principles that connect the properties of physical processes to the properties of experience.[12]

Chalmers declares that the basic principle of consciousness must involve the notion of *information*. He discusses how physically embodied *information states* must be embedded in an *information space* before such states can become actively conscious *knowledge* and, accordingly, transmittable.

> An information space is an abstract object, but following Shannon* we can see information as *physically embodied* when there is a space of distinct physical states, the differences between which can be transmitted down some causal pathway. The transmittable states can be seen as themselves constituting an information space. To borrow a phrase from Bateson (1972), physical information is a *difference which makes a difference.*[13]

For Chalmers, information has two basic aspects, a phenomenal aspect (a subjective experience in time) and a physical aspect (an information space). In this view, information is not information until subjective awareness links with an information space. Yet Chalmers questions whether *all* information requires a subjective (phenomenal) experience. If there is no phenomenal constraint, he speculates, then consciousness as an information space might truly be a fundamental property of the cosmos, and even beyond the cosmos. Chalmers presents a theory that

---

*It was Claude Shannon (a cousin of Thomas Edison) who began what is now called information theory in his 1946 paper that published the equations that link heat flow with information content. Shannon's work led to new ways to encode, modulate, and transfer information signals using different media, from electromagnetic waves to the laser signals that provide a backbone for information flow in the global internet.

identifies a link between information and experience, but then he goes even further, suggesting that "information and experience," or perhaps "experienced information," may be everywhere in the universe, and that perhaps they should be considered as being synonymous with the fundamental ground of being from which all things spring.

> Then experience is much more widespread than we might have believed, as information is everywhere. This is counterintuitive at first, but on reflection the position gains a certain plausibility and elegance . . . . Indeed, if experience is truly a fundamental property, it would be surprising for it to arise only every now and then; most fundamental properties are more evenly spread . . . . Once a fundamental link between information and experience is on the table, the door is opened to some grander metaphysical speculation concerning the nature of the world. . . . The theory I have presented is speculative, but it is a candidate theory.[14]

Chalmers favorably compares his theory to that put forth by John Archibald Wheeler (1911–2008), the quantum physicist who coined the term "black hole."[15] Wheeler, who received his Ph.D. in physics at the age of twenty-one, suggested that information is fundamental to the physics of the universe and regularly proclaimed that he regarded "this idea of information theory as the basis of existence."[16] Wheeler claimed that he could summarize his understanding of the cosmos with the catchphrase "it from bit" and explains how it implies that information may be the basis of the universe.

> It is not unreasonable to imagine that information sits at the core of physics, just as it sits at the core of a computer. Trying to wrap my brain around this idea of information theory as the basis of existence, I came up with the phrase "it from bit."[17]

Wheeler and one of his graduate students, Jacob Bekenstein, went on to calculate the information-storage capacity on the spherical boundary of a black hole and came up with an estimation of astronomical storage capacity, according to which a sphere with the diameter of a typical human blood cell would have the storage capacity of 10^{60} information bits.[18]

Clearly there is some missing link between information and consciousness, and that link should also provide a vehicle or container for the required information space. Thus it is not surprising that some view the electromagnetic field as a space-time carrier of consciousness and Bohm's implicate order as the transcendent container.

ELECTROMAGNETIC FIELDS AS MIND

Several twenty-first-century researchers in the life sciences have concluded that consciousness might have a basis in electromagnetic field phenomena. In 2000, a neurophysiologist in New Zealand, Susan Pockett, published a book hypothesizing that consciousness may very well be the electromagnetic field itself. Pockett states:

> Perhaps the answer we have been looking for is that what has in the past been called the electromagnetic field is itself conscious. And perhaps our individual consciousnesses, which unlike the field as a whole *are* bounded in space and time, are identical with particular local spatiotemporal configurations of the electromagnetic field.[19]

Elsewhere, she states that "the essence of the hypothesis was that conscious experience (a.k.a. sensation) would prove to be identical with certain spatiotemporal patterns in the electromagnetic field"[20] and indicates that perhaps researchers have been looking for consciousness in the wrong ranges of the electromagnetic frequency spectrum.

> The signals we are looking for in brain-generated electromagnetic activity might actually not be in the ELF (extremely low frequency) range where everyone is presently looking, but could turn out to be closer to the microwave frequency range—which is of course always filtered out in present-day electrophysiological recordings.[21]

It is important to note that Pockett assumes consciousness to be, whatever the mechanism or bandwidth, a recent epiphenomenon of some evolutionary process, a serendipitous emergence. This can be seen in her concluding remarks: "The present theory is quite compatible with the view that consciousness was not present in the universe before its biological evolution."[22]

In 2002, Johnjoe McFadden, a professor of molecular genetics at the University of Surrey, put forth a similar theory, the conscious electromagnetic information (CEMI) field theory.[23] McFadden hypothesizes that an electromagnetic information field of the brain is the underlying basis of consciousness. In 2007, McFadden identified *information* as the agential binding element between the physical and the conscious.

> The key feature of the brain's EM [electromagnetic] field is that it is capable of integrating vast quantities of information into a single physical system and it thereby accounts for the binding of consciousness. . . . Unlike quantum theories of consciousness, the CEMI field theory does not require any special physical states in the brains; it is perfectly compatible with brain physiology. Nevertheless, recent work has shown that classical electromagnetic waves may be used to implement quantum algorithms; therefore the brain's CEMI field may be able to perform quantum computations (but without the requirement for quantum coherent states of matter).[24]

Like Pockett, McFadden categorically links consciousness to the electromagnetic field: "I propose that the brain's electromagnetic information field is the physical substrate of conscious awareness."[25] Yet whatever the degree of enthusiasm Pockett and McFadden have for the electromagnetic conjecture, their theory ends there, with no correlative suggestion for further research. The work of brain scientist Karl Pribram, on the other hand, in searching for a neuro-physical basis for memory, also embraced an electromagnetic field theory of consciousness. Relying on his own laboratory research data, Pribram published a theory of consciousness and memory based on the mathematics of the Fourier transform, a practical equation widely used by radio engineers.[26]

It is probable that arbitrary assumptions about consciousness have hampered many researchers; for example, (*a*) the assumption that consciousness is limited specifically to "human consciousness," (*b*) the assumption that there is only one mode or type of consciousness, and (*c*) the assumption that consciousness is only possible in space-time.

Understandably, such assumptions have arisen due to a widespread fascination with hardware in general, and in particular the hardware of the brain, fostered by an approach to science that limits itself to measurements that can be observed in space-time. Thus epiphenomenalism has become mainstream, reinforced by such statements as the following, found in Gerald Edelman and Giulio Tononi's conclusion to their book *A Universe of Consciousness*, where they observe:

> Consciousness, while special, arose as a result of evolutionary innovations in the morphology of the brain and body. The mind arises from the body and its development; it is embodied and therefore part of nature.
>
> We have argued throughout this book that consciousness arises from certain arrangements in the material order of the brain.[27]

If the word *consciousness* in Edelman and Tononi's quote could be replaced with "the mind," or "human mental cognition," the observation might be less problematic, but to state that consciousness arises *from* the brain is questionable. This is a classic example of the proverb "putting the cart before the horse."

We take the opposite view, that it is *consciousness* that is primary and that consciousness predates the emergence of the brain in the evolutionary time scale and also leads brain activity from moment to moment. The brain-mind lags behind consciousness. A growing number of scientifically trained panpsychists refute the following two basic assumptions that seem to be held by nearly all present-day material scientists:

1. That mind is limited to humans and perhaps "the higher animals," and
2. That mind is directly dependent on, or reducible to, the physical substrate of the brain.[28]

Others take the position that consciousness is not limited to space-time, nor is it necessarily limited to human beings. They view the operation of the human "mind" as the operation of consciousness flowing through our physical "meat brains" to process thought and to carry out memory storage and retrieval. Human mental cognition, the coordinated activity of the brain, grows *from out of the primary ground of consciousness*. The following pages support this conjecture that consciousness is *more* fundamental than mental cognition, mental operation.

Nor is consciousness necessarily limited to space, nor restricted in time, nor exclusive to human primates. Descriptions of mystical and religious experiences handed down by every culture provide strong evidence that there exist modes of consciousness that can be explored beyond normal waking thought; all traditions offer prayer, contemplation, and the ingestion of psychotropic plant substances as doorways to experience beyond space and time.[29] Additional evidence is close at hand—the universal nightly human experience of dream states that seem not necessarily to be a product of normally experienced time, space, or mental cognition.

It is evident that serious efforts have indeed been made to explore consciousness in order to discover the outlines of an architecture of consciousness through firsthand experience. In support of such efforts, and to counter the epiphenomenalist turn in consciousness studies, the following pages offer a model of consciousness that builds on the ideas of quantum physicist David Bohm and brain scientist Karl Pribram.[30]

THE PRIBRAM-BOHM HOLOFLUX MODEL

A model of consciousness that supports the observations of Steiner and Patañjali can be found in the Pribram-Bohm holoflux model, a hypothesis that grew from decades of collaboration between Karl Pribram and David Bohm subsequent to their first meeting in the mid-1970s. To express the interconnectedness of this energy flux, spanning a wholeness that embraces both space-time phenomena as well as transcendent phenomena, and at Pribram's suggestion, Bohm settled on the term *holoflux*. In an interview given in 1979, Bohm describes the context of the term *holoflux*.

QUESTION: Could we begin by clarifying the difference between the holomovement, the holograph and the implicate order?

BOHM: Holomovement is a combination of a Greek and Latin word and a similar word would be holokinesis or, still better, *holoflux*, because "movement" implies motion from place to place, whereas flux does not. So, the *holoflux* includes the ultimately flowing nature of what is, and of that which forms therein. The holograph, on the other hand, is merely a static recording of movement, like a photograph: an abstraction from the holomovement. We therefore cannot regard the holograph as anything very basic, since it is merely a way of displaying the holomovement, which latter is, however, the ground of everything, of all that is. The implicate order is the one in which the holomovement takes place, an order that both enfolds and unfolds. Things are unfolded in the implicate order, and that order cannot be entirely expressed in an explicate fashion. Therefore, in this approach, we are not able to go beyond the holomovement or the *holoflux* (the Greek word might be holorhesis, I suppose) although that does not imply that this is the end of the matter.[31]

The Pribram-Bohm model regards consciousness as an energy process, a flow of conscious-information-energy or holoflux energy in the implicate order transforming into electromagnetic field energies in space-time and back, a simultaneous outward flow and an inward flow in "an undivided flowing movement without borders,"[32] continually enriching and informing the entire universe. In the left section of

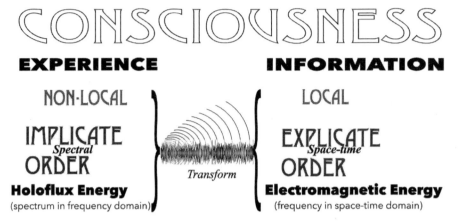

Fig. 7.4. The Pribram-Bohm holoflux model. Adapted from Joye,
"The Pribram–Bohm Holoflux Theory of Consciousness."

figure 7.4, consciousness is expressed as a spectrum of holoflux energy in Bohm's implicate order, and to the right, in the explicate order of space-time, it is expressed as patterned electromagnetic energy.

This holoflux energy resonates with electromagnetic energy of the same frequencies to the right in the diagram, in the space-time region, or explicate order.[33] Viewed from left to right, the diagram reveals a spectrum of holoflux energy in the transcendental implicate order transforming and translating into "things" and "events" in local space-time; and conversely, viewing the diagram from right to left, information generated by "things" and "events" interacting throughout space-time is seen to be transforming (folding) back into the implicate order. This continuous cycle occurs each Planck second and is visualized as the simultaneous flow of information into and energy out from a black hole.

SUPERPOSITION OF CONSCIOUSNESS

Common experience would suggest that all consciousness is consciousness *of* something, such as the experience of a sound, of an image, of a sensation, of an emotion, of an interior verbal thought. These experiences seem to be superpositioned; they often occur at what seems to be the same perceptual moment. Yet each simultaneous stream of experience remains distinct, somehow integrated with all the others. But what is it that is "looking at" this stream of experiences? It is as if there is some meta-consciousness that is more than the sum of each of these individual "experience streams." It is apparent that there must be some other, more comprehensive level, some panoramic perspective that is able to embrace and comprehend them all and that has the amazing ability to *fine-tune* its own selected focus on *one or more* of these streams of awareness while simultaneously dampening and filtering out the many others.

In signal analysis this stream phenomenon is explained by the *superposition principle,* formalized in 1822 by the French mathematician Jean-Baptiste Fourier, who developed the mathematics of what is now called "Fourier analysis" during his search for a mathematical relationship between space-time and frequency.[34] Because signals are more readily superpositioned and manipulated (filtered, amplified, etc.) within the *frequency domain* than in the *time domain,* the Fourier transform equations have become primary and ubiquitous mathematical tools in physics and engineering for analyzing, synthesizing, and transmitting signals between two domains:

1. A "space-time domain (t_d)," and
2. A "frequency domain (f_d)."

Much of electrical-engineering circuit design is done within the frequency domain and only subsequently implemented with time-domain components, as described here by Franklin F. Kuo, chief electrical engineer at the original Bell Telephone Laboratory from which emerged the transistor, the laser, radio astronomy, information theory, and the Unix operating system. In his textbook *Network Analysis and Synthesis*, Kuo states:

We see that in the *time domain* (i.e., where the independent variable is *t*) the voltage-current relationships are given in terms of differential equations. On the other hand, in the complex *frequency domain*, the voltage-current relationships for the elements are expressed in algebraic equations. Algebraic equations are, in most cases, more easily solved than differential equations. Herein lies the raison d'être for describing signals and networks in the frequency domain as well as in the time domain.[35]

Norbert Wiener coined the term *cybernetics* from the Greek κυβερνήτης—"steersman," "governor," "pilot," or "rudder"[36]—during his own work at the same Bell Telephone Laboratory as Kuo. He made use of Fourier's transform to model and analyze brain waves in the frequency domain, where he discovered clear evidence of "self-organization of electroencephalograms or brain waves."[37] Using Fourier analysis, an approach that later became of great interest to Bohm, Wiener was able to detect uniquely narrow frequency ranges, centered within different spatial locations on the cortex, that repeatedly exhibited auto-correlation.[38] Regions on the cortex were identified where specific ranges of frequencies were found to coalesce toward intermediate frequencies, seeming both to attract and to strengthen one another, exhibiting *resonance* or "self-tuning" to amplify and consolidate signals into narrowly specific ranges in the frequency domain f_d.[39] His research led Wiener to conjecture that the *infrared band* of electromagnetic flux may be the loci of "self-organizing systems."

> We thus see that a nonlinear interaction causing the attraction of frequency can generate a self-organizing system, as it does in the case of the brain waves we have discussed. . . . This possibility of self-organization is by no means limited to the very low frequency of these two phenomena. Consider self-organizing systems at the frequency level, say, of infrared light.[40]

Three years after Wiener's 1948 publication of *Cybernetics,* David Bohm stressed the importance of Fourier's equations on the first page of his well-received 646-page textbook, *Quantum Theory,* where he encouraged a familiarity with Fourier analysis for an ontological understanding of quantum phenomena.

It seems impossible, however, to develop quantum concepts extensively without Fourier analysis. It is, therefore, presupposed that the reader is moderately familiar with Fourier analysis.[41]

In order to understand the basic mechanism behind the physics of supersensible perception, it is sufficient to grasp the concept that *frequency vibrations* manifest within two distinct dimensions or domains: a space-time domain and a frequency domain. As we will soon see, these two domains correspond with David Bohm's explicate order (the space-time domain) and implicate order (the frequency domain). Until recently, physicists have focused exclusively within space-time to conduct their research, considering only space and time as having any "reality" in material science and considering the ontological reality of the frequency domain, if at all, in the same vague category as the domain of mathematics itself (i.e., in some unspecified transcendent dimension). Whether there might somehow exist a "real" dimension *outside of* space-time or *beyond* space-time has generally been beyond the purview of the physical sciences. Yet the experienced reality of a region of consciousness beyond space-time is supported by the vast body of firsthand reports generated by religious, mystical, or near-death experiences. In an approach to such experiences, William James, the "father of American psychology," writes:

> The further limits of our being plunge, it seems to me, into an altogether other dimension of existence from the sensible and merely "understandable" world. Name it the mystical region, or the supernatural region, whichever you choose. So far as our ideal impulses originate in this region (and most of them do originate in it, for we find them possessing us in a way for which we cannot articulately account), we belong to it in a more intimate sense than that in which we belong to the visible world, for we belong in the most intimate sense wherever our ideals belong.[42]

Fourier's transform equations (fig. 7.5, page 106) between the two domains of time (t_d) and frequency (f_d) are more than simply

$$f(t) = \int\limits_{-\infty}^{+\infty} X(f)e^{j2\pi ft}\,df \qquad\qquad f(f) = \int\limits_{-\infty}^{+\infty} x(t)e^{-j2\pi ft}\,dt$$

Fourier integral transform of a continuous frequency function into the *time domain* (t_d).

Fourier integral transform of a continuous time function into the *frequency domain* (f_d).

Fig. 7.5. *The Fourier transform and Inverse transform.*
Adapted from Stein and Shakarchi, Fourier Analysis, *134–36.*

mathematical equations, written down as functions in the abstract symbolic language of calculus.[43]

These two expressions indicate that any signal in the space-time domain, *f (time)*, can be transformed into and expressed equivalently as an infinite series of frequency spectra functions, *f (frequency)*, in the frequency domain. The transformation is also possible in the opposite direction, such that any arbitrary signal in the frequency domain, *f (frequency)*, can be transformed into and expressed by an infinite series of time functions, *f (time)*. The two domains mirror one another.

Beyond purely mathematical considerations, the equations can be taken as models of an actual cosmic process (i.e., similar to the way in which Newton's law models the phenomenon of gravity) and they can be understood as mirroring the cosmos in mathematical terms. The model of consciousness presented here proposes that there is indeed an ontological reality to this other region, the frequency domain, and that this region is synonymous with Bohm's "implicate order" as well as Pribram's "holonomic frequency domain."

KARL PRIBRAM'S HOLONOMIC MIND/BRAIN

As a researcher at Stanford, Karl Pribram was one of the first to articulate the idea that the Fourier transform might play a role in brain/mind neuro-physics.[44] Pribram spent decades performing laboratory research to gather experimental data in an effort to solve two mysteries in brain/mind consciousness: (*a*) the location and mechanism of memory storage (the *engram*), and (*b*) the cognitive mechanism behind visual perception.[45] Pribram arrived at the conclusion that the data revealed evidence of Fourier transformations of visual signals from the rods and cones of the eyes and that these Fourier patterns could be detected in spatial Fourier patterns over wide areas of the brain, as fields within the fine-fibered dendritic networks of the cerebral cortex.[46]

In the mid-1960s, Pribram was inspired by reports of the first optical holograms and the empirical evidence that holograms could store, retrieve, and process vast quantities of information using resonant photons in high-frequency beams. In 1971, Pribram published *Languages of the Brain,* in which he detailed his new theory, the holonomic brain/ mind theory, based on evidence of the Fourier transform playing a key role in the mind/brain process. The theory he put forth proposed that the cognitive sensory processes of memory, sight, hearing, and consciousness in general may all operate holographically, in a transformational process of information-coded energies flowing back and forth between space-time and the frequency domain via a Fourier transform mechanism.[47]

Pribram's theory was radical and controversial, challenging two prominent paradigms of modern neuro-physical research: (*a*) the belief that consciousness is an epiphenomenon produced by electrical sparks among synaptic clefts throughout the wiring of neurons in the brain; and (*b*) the belief that somewhere in the physical brain, *engrams* of memory are stored and will eventually be found. Pribram relates a story of a conversation he had at the time, while climbing with colleagues on a hike in Colorado just prior to attending a neuroscience conference in Boulder:

> We had climbed high into the Rocky Mountains. Coming to rest on a desolate crag, a long meditative silence was suddenly broken by a query from Campbell: "Karl, do you really believe it's a Fourier?" I hesitated, and then replied, "No Fergus, that would be too easy, don't you agree?" Campbell sat silently awhile, then said, "You are right, it's probably not that easy. So what are you going to say tomorrow down there?" I replied, this time without hesitation, "That the

transform is a Fourier, of course." Campbell smiled and chortled, "Good for you! So am I."[48]

Pribram's hypothesis was strengthened through a growing appreciation of holography as frequency-superpositioned electromagnetic wave interference.[49] Pribram called his approach "the holonomic brain theory" and postulated the importance of the *frequency domain* in future research.

> Essentially, the theory reads that the brain at one stage of processing performs its analyses in the frequency domain . . . a solid body of evidence has accumulated that the auditory, somatosensory, motor, and visual systems of the brain do in fact process, at one or several stages, input from the senses in the frequency domain.[50]

In Pribram's theory, a pure frequency domain links with the neuronal tissue of the brain through modulating fields of flux within the fine-fibered dendritic webs of the cerebral cortex regions.[51] His paradigm was reinforced at a San Francisco conference during a lecture given by the physicist Geoffrey F. Chew, the head of the UC Berkeley physics department and a former student of Enrico Fermi. Chew presented a conceptual diagram of the Fourier transform process (fig. 7.6) that per-

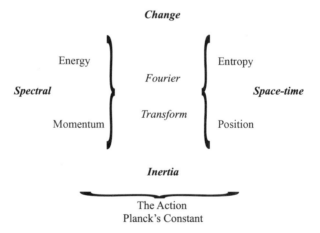

Fig. 7.6. The Dirac-Fourier transform diagram.
Adapted from Pribram, "Consciousness Reassessed."

fectly encapsulated what Pribram had by then become familiar with, the Fourier transform.[52] As shown in the figure, the spectral (frequency) domain, located at the left of the diagram, is directly linked to the space-time domain, depicted at the right, bridged by the Fourier transform, operating at the subatomic levels predicted by Planck's constant.

Pribram asked Chew where he had obtained the diagram and was told that he had been given the diagram by his colleague at Berkeley, the physicist Henry Stapp, who himself said he had been given it directly from the British theoretical physicist Paul Dirac (1902–1984), one of the original founders of quantum mechanics.[53] Whatever the origin of the figure, Pribram chose to include the diagram in several future papers. In "Consciousness Reassessed," Pribram's caption to the figure reads, "The Fourier Transform as the Mediator between Spectral and Spacetime."[54]

In the diagram (fig. 7.6), the spectral domain is shown at the left and space-time to the right, with the Fourier transform between them. The diagram became foundational to Pribram's understanding. It presents a two-way Fourier transform, operational at the boundary between the two domains, located at an event horizon termed in the diagram, "The Action: Planck's Constant." It is this process of turbulent transformation at the event horizon that David Bohm and Basil Hiley termed *holomovement* or *holoflux*.[55]

SPECTRAL FLUX AND THE IMPLICATE ORDER

In 1979, Karl Pribram, at that time a Stanford professor, attended a conference in Cordoba, Spain, where he met David Bohm, a professor of theoretical physics at London University.[56] During the conference, Pribram soon realized that David Bohm's model of the implicate order and its projection, or extrusion into space-time, could be seen as entirely compatible with his own holonomic mind/brain theory.[57] Thus began twenty years of correspondence and dialogue between David Bohm and Karl Pribram, and the two soon became personal friends.

Pribram was encouraged to see in Bohm's theories how frequency-domain information is unfolding as electromagnetic waves into the space-time universe via the Fourier transform. He was also struck by Bohm's description of the cyclical nature of information and energy flowing between the two domains.[58] Even more intriguing was Bohm's belief that "the basic relationship of quantum theory and consciousness is that *they have the implicate order in common.*"[59]

Pribram was equally impressed with Bohm's explanation of nonlocality, a major mystery in quantum physics, which Bohm explains as fundamental to the process of folding and unfolding between explicate and implicate orders, allowing for full superpositioned cohesion of frequency information within the implicate order, and even providing a plausible mechanism for Sheldrake's theories of morphogenetic fields and morphic resonance.

> The implicate order can be thought of as a ground beyond time, a totality, out of which each moment is projected into the explicate order. For every moment that is projected out into the explicate there would be another movement in which that moment would be injected or "introjected" back into the implicate order. If you have a large number of repetitions of this process, you'll start to build up a fairly constant component to this series of projection and injection. That is, a fixed disposition would become established. The point is that, via this process, past forms would tend to be repeated or replicated in the present, and that is very similar to what Sheldrake calls a morphogenetic field and morphic resonance. Moreover, such a field would not be located anywhere. When it projects back into the totality (the implicate order), since no space and time are relevant there, all things of a similar nature might get connected together or resonate in totality. When the explicate order enfolds into the implicate order, which does not have any space, all places and all times are, we might say, merged, so that what happens in one place will interpenetrate what happens in another place.[60]

Bohm's topology is both supported and extended by Pribram's contention, supported by the diagram handed down from Dirac, that the boundary or event horizon between the two domains, where the action occurs, is at the Planck length—precisely where, as Pribram tells us here, spectral density "in-formation" translates into space-time "ex-formation."

> Matter can be seen as an "ex-formation," an externalized (extruded, palpable, compacted) form of flux. By contrast, thinking and its communication (minding) are the consequence of an internalized (neg-entropic) forming of flux, its "in-formation." My claim is that the basis function from which both matter and mind are "formed" is flux (measured as spectral density).[61]

This flux or spectral density is, for Pribram, real, in the same sense that space-time is considered to be real, but this flux is *outside of* or *beyond* space-time. It is in this sense that Pribram made the conceptual leap from considering the Fourier transform as simply a tool of mathematical calculation to a dawning realization that the transform implies the ontological *reality* of a domain *outside of space-time*, a transcendent yet ontologically real domain where energy as flux is "measured as spectral density." Pribram ascertained that Bohm's implicate order is real!

Dirac's original diagram can be extended to include Bohm's two regions of the whole: the implicate order and the explicate order. Figure 7.7 shows this expanded diagram.

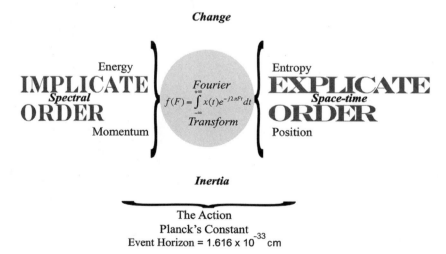

Fig. 7.7. Dirac's Fourier diagram with David Bohm's topology.

Pribram's new interpretation of the diagram is illustrated in figure 7.8, where an iris-like lens of consciousness peers out from the implicate order on the left, projecting the holonomic universe into space-time on the right. This mirrors Karl Pribram's conceptualization of a lens between the two domains, expressed here in *Brain and Perception*.

> These two domains characterize the input to and output from a lens that performs a Fourier transform. On one side of the transform lies the space-time order we ordinarily perceive. On the other side lies a distributed enfolded holographic-like order referred to as the frequency or spectral domain.[62]

Note that the image of an iris in the diagram appears at the edge of the event horizon of a quantum black hole, or implicate order holosphere. The iris symbolizes consciousness looking *out* from the implicate order *into* space-time via a Fourier transform lensing process. This approach to a topology of consciousness as something that is

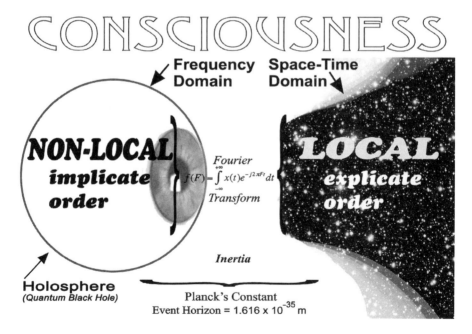

Fig. 7.8. Topology of consciousness in Pribram's diagram.

looking out and seeing itself is supported here by the mathematician George Spencer-Brown in *Laws of Form*:

> Now the physicist himself, who describes all this, is, in his own account, constructed of it. He is, in short, made of a conglomeration of the very particulars he describes, no more, no less, bound together by and obeying such general laws as he himself has managed to find and record. Thus we cannot escape the fact that the world we know is constructed in order (and thus in such a way as to be able) to see itself. This is indeed amazing. Not so much in view of what it sees, although this may appear fantastic enough, but in respect of the fact that it can see at all. . . . But in order to do so, evidently it must first cut itself up into at least one state which sees, and at least one other state which is seen. In this condition it will always partially elude itself.[63]

COSMOLOGY AND THE IMPLICATE ORDER

In 1980, Bohm published *Wholeness and the Implicate Order*, and in a section in which he discusses the cosmology of the implicate order, he puts forth a solution to the problem of "zero-point" energy by regarding the Planck length as the shortest wavelength possible:

> If one were to add up the energies of all the "wave-particle" modes of excitation in any region of space, the result would be infinite, because an infinite number of wavelengths is present. However, there is good reason to suppose that one need not keep on adding the energies corresponding to shorter and shorter wavelengths. There may be a certain shortest possible wavelength, so that the total number of modes of excitation, and therefore the energy, would be finite. . . . When this length is estimated it turns out to be about 10^{-35} m.[64]

Bohm brings up the school of Parmenides and Zeno, which held that all of space is actually a plenum, and he points out that as recently as the last century this same theory was presented in the widely accepted hypothesis of the *ether*.[65] Bohm describes how there is a "holo-movement" in this immense sea of "zero-point energy" to be understood as an "undivided flowing movement without borders," and he goes on to state:

> It is being suggested here, then, that what we perceive through the senses as empty space is actually the plenum, which is the ground for the existence of everything, including ourselves. The things that appear to our senses are derivative forms and their true meaning can be seen only when we consider the plenum, in which they are generated and sustained, and into which they must ultimately vanish.[66]

Bohm's vision is that of a vast plenum of holospheres, a holoplenum, filling every position within the space-time boundaries of our cosmos (fig. 7.9).

This holoplenum of holospheres in the Pribram-Bohm cosmology is visualized as the boundary interface between the explicate space-time domain and the nonlocal, nontemporal implicate domain. In this map

Fig. 7.9. The holoplenum of holospheres. Copyright J. R. Bale, Balefire Communications.

can be found an answer to the "hard problem of consciousness" posed by Chalmers, for it is from *within* each holosphere that consciousness is "peering out," while at the same time "projecting" the space-time explicate order that we experience with many of our sensory systems. Here Bohm summarizes his cosmological essay by proposing that "consciousness is to be comprehended in terms of the implicate order, along with reality as a whole" and stating unequivocally that "the implicate order is also its primary and immediate actuality."[67]

It is not surprising to discover that Bohm's model is quite similar to the view of the German mathematician and philosopher Gottfried Wilhelm Leibniz (1646–1716), best known for his theory of monads.[68] Leibniz proposed that the universe is made up of an infinite number of simple substances known as monads. Each monad is unique and is not affected by time, being a center of force, a force that Leibniz tells us projects the phenomena of space, matter, and motion. Unlike atoms, monads possess no material or spatial character, yet each follows a pre-programmed set of "instructions" unique to its own position in the universal plenum. Leibniz goes on cryptically to tell us that each human being constitutes a monad.

This geometrical image of a universe of monads is also supported by the mathematician/philosopher Alfred North Whitehead (1861–1947), who envisions a plenum of "actual entities" making up the manifest universe. According to Whitehead in his most important book, *Process and Reality* (1929), nothing exists in the universe more basic then actual entities. They exist as the foundational substrata, or plenum, from which space-time is projected outward. With one exception, Whitehead tells us, all actual entities lie within the space-time domain. These he calls "occasions of experience." The single exception lying outside of space-time, according to Whitehead, is the "atemporal actual entity," which he clearly identifies as God.

Going back to an earlier millennium than Bohm, Whitehead, and Leibniz, back to the third century BCE, we find Aristotle, who held that the reason an apple falls to the ground is because it seeks its natural

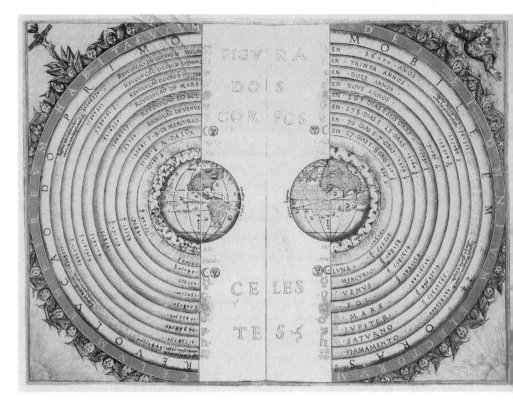

Fig. 7.10. Bartolomeu Velho's Ptolemaic geocentric conception of the universe. First published in Cosmographia, *1568.*

place at the center of the universe. Aristotle set forth a geocentric model based on the following three propositions:

1. The Earth is positioned at the center of the universe.
2. The Earth is fixed (nonmoving) in relation to the rest of the universe.
3. The Earth is special and unique compared to all other heavenly bodies.[69]

This Aristotelian geocentric model of the universe can be seen depicted in figure 7.10, a vision of the universe according to the sixteenth-century Portuguese cosmographer and cartographer Bartolomeu Velho.

Substituting "holosphere" for "Earth" in Aristotle's propositions, each Planck holosphere can be taken as positioned at the center of the universe, each holosphere is fixed (nonmoving) in relation to all other holospheres in the holoplenum, and each holosphere is "special" by virtue of its unique Hilbert space coordinates.[70]

The cosmology of consciousness developed in this chapter visually maps an ocean of radiant energies filling the known cosmos of 2 trillion galaxies from a grand diameter of 8.8×10^{26} meters (and expanding) down to the bottom of space at 1.6×10^{-35} meter (the Planck length limit).[71] While defying conventional logic, the distance to the farthest edge from any point in the universe is everywhere the same, 4.4×10^{26} meters, and it is from the omnipresent center (i.e., the implicate order as a plenum of holospheres) that our map reveals the primary consciousness of Self peering out into its universe of space-time at every point. As our vision begins to open to these astounding galactic dimensions from both within and without our own bodies, our sense of being connected to a vast network of awareness increases, growing to the point at which we sense we are being warmly welcomed to join this galactic "inner-net" that clearly dwarfs the range of connections currently found in our small Earth's "inter-net."

The next chapter enhances our map by adding a useful overlay to the material thus far discussed. Chapter 8 presents an overview of the physiological basis of consciousness that indicates feasible areas and mechanisms whereby human consciousness may function within the human body. It is hoped that this additional orientation will encourage the psychonaut, standing on the threshold of supersensible perception, to "dive within."

8

The Physiology of Consciousness

The previous chapter developed the theory that the ground of consciousness, consciousness itself, manifests as a continuous flow of energy in a two-way inward/outward transformation between two domains through a boundary that is timeless and omnipresent. This energy was described as being encoded with both information and meaning, flowing between our familiar space-time and a nonspatial, nontemporal transcendent domain that David Bohm termed the implicate order, located at the center, everywhere. To express the interconnectedness of this energy flow, spanning a wholeness that embraces both space-time phenomena as well as transcendent phenomena, Bohm selected the term *holoflux*. In this chapter we develop further details of the holoflux model to understand how consciousness functions within the human body so that contemplatives may more quickly master the operation of previously unsuspected systems of direct supersensible awareness.

THE HOLOFLUX THEORY OF CONSCIOUSNESS

The holoflux theory rests on two fundamental paradigms: Karl Pribram's holonomic brain theory and David Bohm's ontological interpretation of quantum theory.[1] These theories have been shown to be congruent, supported and knit together by established principles of electrical-communication engineering. As described in chapter 7, the holoflux theory discussed here can be better understood by examining the following nine propositions:

- *A centered cosmos:* In agreement with the theory of general relativity, the holoflux theory is founded on the notion that the universe has a center and that center is everywhere.

- *Holoflux:* Dark energy of the implicate order, outside of space-time; it can be considered to be Karl Pribram's theorized flux within David Bohm's implicate order, and it is an energy of sentient awareness that views the outwardly explicate world of space-time from within an implicate order.[2]

- *Quantum black holes:* Quantum black holes are *Planck holospheres* of the Bohmian implicate order; gateway portals into the implicate order, they are bounded by spherical shells, each of Planck-length diameter (10^{-35} meter).

- *The holoplenum:* An invariant *holoplenum* of close-packed holospheres or *Planck isospheres*, underlying and from which is projected the explicate order; the holoplenum fills a continuum of isospheres everywhere in the physical universe from the center of each position in space-time; the concept had been intuited by Leibniz in his theory of monads.

- *Resonance:* Holoflux frequency-resonance complementarity connects the explicate order (the outside world) with the implicate order (the inside world); holoflux resonance occurs everywhere between the implicate order (frequency-phase flux in the implicate order, f_i) and isospheres of the explicate order in spherical shells. These holo-shells would manifest at corresponding distances, λ_i, from each central Planck holosphere, to maintain the relationship, $f_i \lambda_i = c$, where c is the speed of light in a vacuum, approximately 3×10^8 m/sec.

- *Cyclic process:* A flowing movement, an *electromagnetic-holoflux* movement of energy continually cycles between the implicate order and the explicate order; the flow can be mathematically modeled through Fourier transforms and the Bohm quantum potential wave functions.

- *A cosmic clock:* Granular units of Planck time (t_P) vibrate at a "clock-cycle" rate of 5.39106×10^{44} cycles per second, synchronizing the flow between alternating manifestations of implicate and explicate frequency information; in Cartesian coordinates, this can be pictured as a square wave, a Planck-time clock.

- *Bohm's quantum potential function:* Conceptional computations within the implicate order are "expressed" in space-time (the explicate order) via the effect of Bohm's quantum potential function, *Q*, a concept pioneered in de Broglie's "pilot wave" paradigm of 1927.

- *A Fourier lens:* The Fourier-type mathematical transform can be seen to act as a lens through which the implicate "views" or "cognizes" the explicate order of space-time; this Fourier lensing is the process by which the implicate order observes, retrieves, and projects information generated within the explicate order.

A diagram of these nine propositions is presented in figure 8.1, in which congruent concepts of five contemporary pioneering philosophers of consciousness studies are contextually positioned.

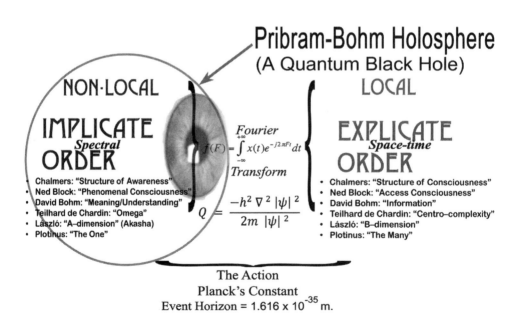

Fig. 8.1. Solving the hard problem of consciousness.

- David Chalmers's (1995) "structure of awareness" is posited to be synonymous with the implicate order, and his "structure of consciousness" accordingly is shown within the explicate order.
- Ned Block's (1995) "phenomenal (qualia) consciousness" lies in the implicate order, and his "access (sensory) consciousness" in the explicate order.
- David Bohm's (1980) "meaning" lies in the implicate order, and his "information" in the explicate order.
- Pierre Teilhard de Chardin's (1956) "Omega" lies in the implicate order, and his "centro-complexity" in the explicate order.
- Laszlo's (2014) "A-dimension" lies in the implicate order, and his "B-dimension" lies in the explicate order.[3]

COSMOLOGICAL PROCESS AS PLASMA DISPLAY

The holonomic process underlying the Bohmian "Whole" may be more easily visualized by considering a holoplenum of quantum black holes, or Planck holospheres, located spatially at the center, everywhere, but close-packed and thus filling everything, the absolute ground of space. Beneath the infinitely thin film surface of each holosphere lies the nondual implicate order. Surrounding and radiating outward from each Planck holosphere throughout space are spherical shells of quantum potential, infinitely thin information-encoded shells of holoflux energy, each separated from its next inner shell, like nested Russian dolls, by the quantum exclusion radial distance of one Planck length. These infinitely thin isospheric shells of holoflux extend outward to the current maximum diameter of the universe itself. The diameter of the universe expands outward at a fixed rate, the speed of light, as it continuously generates new holoflux shells that store ever more information while the universe expands and collects experience.

We can now visualize an almost infinite series of nested shells surrounding each central Planck holosphere. These holospheres and their shells consist of "implicate order stuff," or holoflux. They are the framework of space-time, but they are not of it.

The global panoramic intersection of these holospheric shells manifests as the projection of the holonomic universe into space-time. The cumulative effect of this projection, as regarded by human physicists observing from significantly higher scalar dimensions, is described as "matter." The phenomenon can be understood as a *process of projected creation*, an omnipresent, ongoing holographic extrusion of information *from* the implicate order *into* the explicate order, where the various structures of the cosmos (galactic clusters, stars, etc.), the complex unfoldings *into* space-time, are perceived by the human eye and mind to be three-dimensional, when they are actually holographic projections *from* the implicate order, from the center outward into our cosmos of space-time.

Another way of visualizing the projected illusion of space-time reality from the holoplenum is by expanding on the metaphor of a flat-panel plasma display (such as the one you may be viewing as you read this).

Consider the human visual threshold for detecting separate images, which lies somewhere between 10 to 12 images per second; the industry standard in the motion picture industry is 24 frames per second.[4] This standard ensures that the presentation of a sequence of projected images will appear to a human viewer as a smooth and continuous motion.

By contrast, if the entire universe flashes in and out of existence at the clock-cycle rate of the Planck-time constant of 5.3×10^{-44} seconds; this is equivalent to a "frame" rate of almost 10^{44} "frames per second," and thus the cosmos would *appear* to be smooth and continuous in all respects even to an electron, and certainly to any human observer of the cosmos, even at quantum dimensions.

The approximate image resolution of a "holoplenum display" obtained by dividing one inch by the Planck length yields a maximum resolution of 1.584×10^{34} holopixels per inch. At such hyperfine resolution, even a Higgs boson in the 10^{-17} meter dimensional range would appear to be moving smoothly through space.

HOLONOMIC STORAGE:
THE BEKENSTEIN BOUND

In *Wholeness and the Implicate Order*, Bohm articulates and develops a "quantum potential"[5] function that projects the explicate space-time universe out from within an enfolded sub-quantum implicate order. Bohm's quantum potential function is congruent with de Broglie's pilot-wave theory of 1927, as both are based on a conviction that there exist "hidden variables" in sub-quantum regions not accessible to observational exploration using current material-science technology (and far beyond the capabilities of the CERN Large Hadron Collider).

Both the de Broglie pilot-wave theory and Bohm's quantum potential[6] (known as "Q") are attempts to account for sub-quantum effects issuing from an implicate order in a domain of "hidden variables" far below the observational capabilities of contemporary material science.

Both theories account for the cybernetic processing of information, simultaneously being cycled from the space-time world and enfolded into the non-dual frequency domain where the accumulating information is processed nonlocally within the implicate order. Driven then by the implicate order, a pilot wave of quantum potential nudges the configurations in space-time into an altered, slightly new configuration, much as a small tugboat might influence an enormous freighter. If the cosmos operates at its maximum possible clock cycle, as discussed previously, this pilot wave might be seen to operate at the extreme clock-cycle rate of the Planck-time constant, or 10^{44} Hz.

But exactly how does the implicate order affect the explicate order, or rather, what might be the cybernetic mechanism of control and communication? Consider one complete clock-cycle of creation (occurring at the rate of 10^{+44} seconds per cycle). At the beginning of the cycle, the cosmos consists of a vast accumulation of stored information distributed everywhere. At each cycle this information is immediately "read" into the implicate order where it is digested and processed outside of time and space. The next phase of this cybernetic cycle finds the implicate order sending out subatomic "Q" pilot waves everywhere to nudge the universe into its newly computed configuration. This entire process has been visualized metaphorically as the ouroboric snake eating its own tail (fig. 7.2 on page 91.) But where in space-time is data stored at these sub-quantum levels?

One possibility is to consider the information-storage potential of an isosphere encoded with granular "bits" of data. In 1970, Jacob D. Bekenstein proposed that there must be an absolute maximum amount of information that can be stored in a finite region of space. Using the Planck constants he showed how these fundamentals of quantum physics can be used to determine this limit.[7] Twenty years later, Bekenstein's theory, now widely known as "the Bekenstein Bound," was extended into what is called the *holographic principle* by Leonard Susskind, who described how information within any volume of space can be holographically encoded on the surface of a black hole bounding the region.[8] A description of this configuration is presented here by Wheeler himself, as first related to him by Bekenstein:

> One unit of entropy (information), one unit of randomness, one unit of disorder, Bekenstein explained to me, must be associated with a bit of area of this order of magnitude (a Planck length square). . . . Thus one unit of entropy is associated with each 1.04×10^{-69} square meters of the horizon of a black hole.[9]

This proposed upper limit to the information that can be contained on the surface of a specific, finite volume of space has come to be known as the Bekenstein Bound,[10] a geometric depiction of the arrangement of information bits, or "qubits," stored on the bounding surface of a spherical volume, black hole, or isosphere.

This same topological approach to data storage can be applied to human physiology. Using a well-known biological structure as an example, it is possible to calculate the maximum memory-storage capacity of an isosphere the size of a single erythrocyte, the ubiquitous red blood cell found throughout the human body. Using Wheeler's approach to determine the number of Bekensteinian equivalent data bits (qubits) on the surface of a red blood cell and using the average diameter of a typical human erythrocyte of 8.1 microns (or 8.1×10^{-5} m), the maximum possible storage capacity on the spherical shell around a single cell can be calculated.[11] To obtain this limiting number of bits, the surface area on a spherical shell 8.1 microns in diameter must be divided by 1.04×10^{-69} square meter (which is the Bekenstein unit of entropy, or approximately the square of the Planck length of 1.616199×10^{-35}). The surface area of this erythrocyte-bisected sphere according to this calculation is $4\pi r^2$ or $4\pi(4.05 \times 10^{-5})^2 = 4\pi(1.64 \times 10^{-9}) = 1.64 \times 10^{-9}$ square meter. Dividing this by the qubit area of 1.04×10^{-69} square meter yields an estimated maximum storage capacity of 1.6×10^{60} qubits of storage space for potential information encoding. This is an extremely large data-storage capacity, considerably larger than, by contrast, the entire capacity of the National Security Agency's Utah Data Center, which has been designed to have a maximum data-storage capacity of twelve exabytes or 12×10^{18} bytes.[12] What this tells us is that even a single human red blood cell has the electronic capacity to store an immense amount of information, more than the largest computer storage system currently devised.

UNFOLDING THE IMPLICATE INTO SPACE-TIME

Waveguides and the Topology of Human Consciousness
Bohm's approach to consciousness is radical indeed. As revealed in the Pribram-Bohm holoflux theory, Bohm explored deeper dimensions of space than had ever been attempted by physicists who study particles in the 10^{-15} meter range. Bohm's implicate order lay far deeper at the very bottom of space, at the Planck range of 10^{-35} meter.[13]

What are the implications of this model for human consciousness, cognitively operational at temporal and spatial scales vastly larger than those found at these sub-quantum Planck boundaries? To answer this we must first complete the Pribram-Bohm cosmological topology of consciousness, and to do this the concept of isospheres, shells within shells, must be considered. Moving outwardly, radially, from the interior bounding event horizon at each central Planck holosphere can be identified isospheric shells of the implicate order, extruding into space at exact Planck length (quantum) intervals.

This series of concentric shells, each one separated from the next by one Planck length, are infinitely thin shells of the implicate order (see fig. 8.2); they extrude into space and they intersect in space with other shells bounding other Planck holospheres to project the entire holographic universe. It is the cumulative interference effect of the intersection of individual isospheric shells that project images at higher scales, holographically, into three-dimensional space.

Each isospheric shell, as Bekenstein determined, has a potentially enormous storage capacity in "qubits" of information encoded on the event horizon bounding each shell, depending only on the radius of the shell within the range from 10^{-35} to 10^{27} meters.[14] Accessible simultaneously in both the implicate order and the explicate order, such encoded information provides the data to guide evolving forms as they project into the explicate via the pilot-wave mathematics of Bohm's "many-dimensioned quantum potential."[15] As part of this process, in-formation becomes ex-formation as the implicate order unfurls into the explicate.

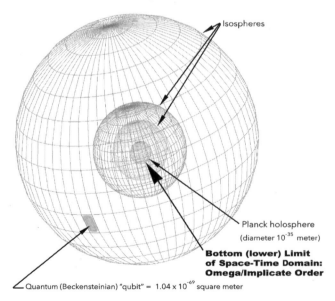

Fig. 8.2. Topological model of isospheres surrounding a Planck holosphere.

The plasmatic forms appearing in space-time as electromagnetic flux energy are mirrored by and resonate within the implicate order as the dark energy of frequency-phase holoflux.

This cosmic geometry of the Pribram-Bohm model offers a framework for omnipresent two-way portals, direct gateways linking the explicate and the implicate. Here, the deep consciousness of the universe flows in a cyclic, cybernetic, perhaps fractal movement in time and space, moving through an endless, bidirectional process, with consciousness itself involved in a dance of transformation.

How then does this topology support human consciousness, thought, and perception in space-time? How can electromagnetic-frequency plasma in space-time resonate with holoflux plasma in the implicate order? First of all, the energies must be within the same frequency range in order for maximum interactive resonance to occur. Where the frequencies overlap as they superimpose and interpenetrate one other, resonance occurs.

Resonance is a naturally occurring phenomenon characteristic of physical objects or plasma fields extended in space-time. The resonance effect is seen when objects or complex signal systems exhibit remarkable sensitivity to particular external frequencies flowing in, through, and around the system, frequencies that approach the "natural resonant frequency" of the object or signal system; perfect resonance occurs when the input frequency and the natural frequency are identical.[16] This principle of resonance governs all cybernetic feedback loops and is a key factor in the design of antennas for electromagnetic transmitting and receiving systems. The goal of antenna design is to construct an antenna that is maximally resonant within a specific narrow frequency range of incoming (external or internal) electromagnetic radiation; when the input frequency and the natural frequency of the antenna coincide or move significantly close to one another, resonance occurs. This simplest and most common antenna design is the dipole antenna, which depends directly on the size (wavelength) of the incoming electromagnetic wave. A dipole antenna is designed to be physically half the size of the incoming wavelength, as described here in a textbook of antenna design.

A fundamental form of an antenna: length is approximately equal
to half the transmitting wavelength. It is the unit from which many
more complex forms of antennas are constructed. It is known as a
dipole antenna.[17]

This same half-wavelength effect governs the design of network communication waveguides applied to fiber optics in the internet, where the
antenna is the fiber channel itself acting as a waveguide. The waveguide
is highly efficient for two reasons: first, as its name implies, the waveguide guides the electromagnetic wave within its channel with maximum
efficiency; and second, it shields the signal in the channel from external
electromagnetic waves. The inner diameter of the hollow waveguide is
designed to be equal to exactly half the wavelength of the electromagnetic
energy signal shielded by and flowing through the waveguide channel.

Waveguides have been used for over a century both commercially
and in research to channel and guide vibrating energy in specific limited
frequency ranges; the fiber-optic networks hosting the global internet
operate on this principle, channeling electromagnetic radiation at fixed
laser frequencies.[18] It was discovered late in the nineteenth century that
circular metallic tubes, or hollow metal ducts, similar to A/C ventilation
ducts but much smaller, could be used to channel and guide either sound
vibrations in air or electromagnetic energy in air or in a vacuum. Without
the waveguide, the vibrational energy field would fan out in all directions,
like the rays of the sun emerging from a single central location. When
waves of vibrating electromagnetic energy are not focused and condensed
into a single specific direction, their power is greatly reduced. This energy
disperses outwardly, the magnetic vectored arrowheads pushing into the
inside of an infinitely expanding sphere. A waveguide, however, constrains
the magnetic component of the wave front of vibrating energy to one specific linear direction, in parallel with the center of the waveguide, and
thus the confined wave itself loses very little power while it propagates
along the central axis of the waveguide—like a stream of water emerging
from the pinprick of a large, taut, water balloon.[19]

The most common type of fiber-optic cable used in the internet has a core diameter of 8 to 10 micrometers and is designed for use in the near infrared.[20] The electromagnetic-signal wavelength that runs through the global fiber-optic network is powered by highly efficient carbon dioxide lasers and has a wavelength of 10 micrometers. Coincidentally (or not?), the average human blood capillary diameter is also 10 microns, and blood capillaries are at all times full of carbon dioxide.

Dimensional analysis and a cursory examination of human physiology would immediately suggest two candidates for waveguide systems within the human body: (*a*) the blood capillary system, and (*b*) the microtubule system. The corresponding resonant frequency for electromagnetic waves using such waveguides corresponds to wavelengths matching the inner diameter of these structures. For blood-system capillaries, this corresponds to radiation with a wavelength of 9.3 to 10.0 microns, the average inner diameter of a capillary. For microtubules, the radiation wavelength would be found in a range of 40 nanometers, the inner diameter of the microtubule waveguides. Figure 8.3, on page 130, depicts the location of each of these potential waveguide frequency bands within a wider section of the electromagnetic spectrum.

There is no impediment to our blood acting as an electromagnetic plasma within the capillary system, and, as previously mentioned, the opening page of a textbook on plasma physics reads, "It has often been said that 99% of the matter in the universe is in the plasma state."[21]

In such a model, the entire blood system within the human body can be considered to be acting as an extensively polarized "super cell" of nonlocal electromagnetic plasma energy, which can then be differentiated from the neuronal brain body of consciousness, itself generated by sequential electrical impulse-driven patterns flowing in the nervous system. Moving charges generate magnetic fields, and ionized human blood flow is no exception: flowing blood plasma results in the creation of a magnetic field, and this is in accord with the conjecture of QBD.[22]

The circulatory system can be seen as a magnetic plasma composed primarily of ionized red blood cells (erythrocytes) and water molecules, flowing together in complex vortices of blood plasma around every cell and through every capillary of the body.[23] Each erythrocyte is a flexible, annular, biconcave disk shaped like a doughnut (in geometry, a torus), having a thin webbed center where the hole in a pastry doughnut would be located. The typical outside diameter of a red blood cell is approximately 9 microns, close to the infrared wavelength of 9.6 microns generated by the human body.[24] The adult human body contains approximately 6 grams of iron, of which 60 percent is stored throughout the 10^{12} erythrocytes, each of which contains approximately 270 million atoms of ionic iron embedded within transparent hemoglobin in a

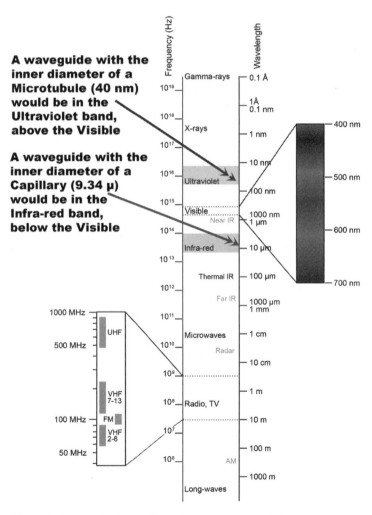

Fig. 8.3. Microtubules and capillaries as waveguides.
Annotations by author; graphic by Jahoe.

toroidal locus.[25] Thus each erythrocyte, replete with iron ions embedded in hemoglobin, creates, in effect, an ionized iron toroid.[26]

Recent studies have also discovered neuronal generation of electromagnetic energy in the near-infrared region of the spectrum centered around 10 microns. Radiation emission was repeatedly measured emanating from live crab neurons in extremely narrow, discrete spectral bands within the frequency range corresponding to a spectral region from 10.5 to 6.5 microns.[27]

The implications of this model are considerable: there may exist in nature a unique resonant frequency for each individual human being. It is useful here to step through a topological analysis of the possible functions of a human red blood cell, given its geometry, as a locus of consciousness, and the possible use of the erythrocyte as a locus of memory storage at human biological scales. If, as previously conjectured, the red blood cell has an ideal diameter to resonate electromagnetic radiation in its ferrite-embedded ring at the human infrared wavelength of 10 microns, then it is reasonable to ask if this configuration could accommodate a single unique isospheric frequency (wavelength) for each of the currently seven billion living humans on the planet. In other words, does this geometry allow for the possibility of each human being also having a single unique frequency within the infrared electromagnetic radiation that resonates within the human cardiovascular waveguide system? Figure 8.4 on page 132 outlines the topological feasibility of this approach.

Assuming each unique frequency would match its radially unique isosphere, separated by only one Planck length, figure 8.4 suggests how seven billion unique isospheres, each of quantum discrete frequency, might be nested within the geometry of a typical human red blood cell (in the image, a multiple of seven billion times the Planck length of approximately 10^{-35} m results in an estimated shell thickness of 10^{-26} m). This model supports the feasibility that each living human being might have a unique holospheric frequency, detectable by other human blood cells via the implicate order, about which each is centered. This would provide a possible mechanism for communication, via the properties of resonance, nonlocality, and superposition in the frequency domain of the implicate order.

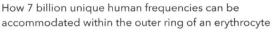

How 7 billion unique human frequencies can be
accommodated within the outer ring of an erythrocyte

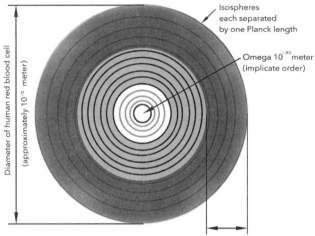

Fig. 8.4. Isospheric capacity of a single erythrocyte.
Adapted from Joye, "The Pribram-Bohm Holoflux Theory."

TWO PRIMARY MODES OF CONSCIOUSNESS

We human beings tend to assume that there is only one single consciousness that we experience, but is this actually true? Are we experiencing the same variety of consciousness while solving mathematical puzzles, making love, praying, drinking ourselves to the point of inebriation, dancing, or experiencing entheogens? The Pribram-Bohm map of consciousness claims that there are two quite distinct modes of consciousness operating simultaneously within the human being: an *explicate* mode of consciousness (operating in space-time) and an *implicate* mode of consciousness (operating in a transcendent domain outside of space-time). A clear distinction between the two varieties of consciousness was made, independently, by the highly educated introspective psychonauts Pierre Teilhard de Chardin and Rudolf Steiner. Based on decades of personal observation and thought, they each have come to the same conclusion, that there are two primary modes of human consciousness.[28]

Teilhard describes consciousness as having an *axial* component and a *tangential* component. At the conclusion of his essay "The Activation of Human Energy," Teilhard summarizes his understanding that the energy behind these two modes "are two different energies—one axial, increasing, and irreversible, and the other peripheral or tangential, constant, and reversible: and these two energies are linked together in 'arrangement.'"[29] According to Teilhard, that which he terms *tangential* consciousness is generated by the sequential firing of electrical pulses among physical neurons in the brain. In contrast to this tangential brain consciousness that empowers our linear verbal thinking, space-time awareness, and sense of individuality, Teilhard's *axial* consciousness, which he occasionally refers to as "soul" or "spirit" (perhaps to satisfy Vatican criticism of his ideas), is also, he tells us, "a new dimensional zone" that brings with it "new properties."[30] It is this very same *axial* consciousness—the mode that Rudolf Steiner refers to as *radial* consciousness—that can be consciously explored through the development of supersensible perception.

Teilhard describes how increasing the centration of consciousness along the radial component leads to a state of "being mentally ultra-humanized by self-compression."[31] This is clearly reminiscent of Patañjali's teaching of dhyāna, whereby a sustained concentration of consciousness will lead directly to an abrupt transformation of consciousness into the state of samādhi (supersensible perception). Teilhard, in words again similar to Patañjali's, tells us that at "a certain *critical point of centration*" of consciousness, directed inwardly toward a central region that he calls the Omega point (Bohm's implicate order), a condition of "self-reflection occurs."[32]

To better understand what Teilhard means by increasing the centration of consciousness along the radial component, a visual metaphor may be helpful. Visualize an ice skater beginning to spin in place. As the ice skater slowly bends her elbows, drawing in her arms closer to the axis of her body, her spin accelerates. Likewise, as a contemplative begins to focus awareness radially inward during meditation (dhyāna), compressing the region of awareness ever closer to a central focal point (this could be, for example, the center of the heart, or the center of the cranium, throat, perineum, or fontanelle), the energy of consciousness steadily increases its spin frequency about the region of focus. Another example can be seen in a magnifying glass focusing the sun's rays to the point of ignition as the condensed rays generate heat. If the contemplative is able to maintain this focus (dhyāna) for a sustained period (dhāraṇā), the condensed energy will begin to resonate at higher frequencies as it encompasses smaller and smaller regions (note how this same inverse relation is found in electromagnetic fields, whereby smaller wavelengths manifest higher frequencies and higher energies). After a short time, the focal point of the magnifying glass will ignite into a flame. Similarly, after a short period of sustained contemplation within a single region, the contemplative's consciousness will soon ignite a state of samādhi, the gateway to supersensible perception.

In a strikingly similar way, Rudolf Steiner describes the two modes of consciousness in his discussion of the human physiology of consciousness. He provides a description, replete with diagrams, of how our consciousness is driven by "nerve-activity" that operates "at right angles to" a radial consciousness located within the "blood-activity" of the circulatory system."[33] Steiner goes so far as to tell us that the *radial mode* of consciousness operates *within the blood system*.[34] Thus both Steiner and Teilhard agree there is definitely a second mode of consciousness beyond that of the "nerve-activity" of neuronal brain activity and that a second mode of consciousness at right angles to brain consciousness operates in an axial or radial mode.

How do these two modes of Teilhard and Steiner accord with the Pribram-Bohm model we have discussed? Ordinary human consciousness, the daily experience of awareness by human beings who are not sleeping, can be identified with the nerve activity of the brain. This brain consciousness manifests, according to Pribram after decades of research,[35] in an electromagnetic plasma field located among the thin dendritic regions of the cerebral cortex.

This is the "consciousness" examined in experiments conducted by Benjamin Libet, whose research revealed that human awareness of an "intention to act" *lagged behind* the actual EEG-measured "readiness

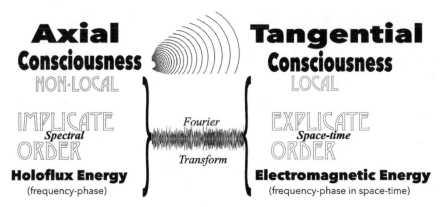

Fig. 8.5. The two modes of consciousness.

potential" by an average of 200 milliseconds.[36] Unfortunately, this evidence supported a current, erroneous, widely held view among neurophysiologists that consciousness is some type of an epiphenomenon, a fortuitous byproduct of neuronal activity. This epiphenomenal view is correct only if one mode of consciousness is being considered—the mode that Teilhard called "tangential," the same mode that Steiner referred to as "nerve-activity," a recent result of evolutionary growth and transformation within the brain.

The actual situation is more sophisticated according to Pribram and Bohm, who see two modes of consciousness functioning simultaneously as depicted in figure 8.5, where the Teilhard/Steiner axial consciousness is seen to "peer out from" the transcendent implicate order, shown on the left of the figure, *into* our more familiar explicate space-time order on the right. Not only is this implicate order consciousness peering out into space-time, but it is also simultaneously *projecting* the configuration of material reality into our space-time cosmos. Because nerve activity within space-time requires the relatively slow processing of physiological systems in the time dimension, brain consciousness activity lags *behind* implicate order consciousness. Given the relatively slow time requirements for the various operations within the sensory and memory systems of the human body, Libet found there to be an average 200 millisecond delay *after* the primary conscious awareness of the implicate order.

Libet's discovery puzzled brain scientists,[37] but can be understood as the delay between thought and a primary mode of awareness that is "before thought," a mode of consciousness outside of time, one that dwells in the immediacy of the implicate order.

> To dwell in the present moment requires not dwelling in thought, because thought takes duration and is a slow process. What is needed is not to deny thought, but to find the part of our experiencing which occurs before each thought.[38]

AN EXPERIMENTAL SEARCH
FOR CONSCIOUSNESS

The model of consciousness discussed in this book provides a feasible solution to the Chalmers (1995) "hard problem of consciousness."[39] If consciousness is considered to be manifesting as energy flow in electromagnetic-frequency fields, then one should be able to determine experimentally the location of high bandwidth information networks within the human body. Such bandwidths must provide the data-network infrastructure through which electromagnetic information interchange guides the growth process, effects repair, and catalyzes evolutionary mutation. The widespread assumption of contemporary neuroscience has been that consciousness emerges from neuronal activity in the human brain only as an epiphenomenon.[40] Accordingly, we should search for a frequency range most likely to carry high-bandwidth electromagnetic (radio) waves within structures of the human body.

THE FREQUENCY RANGE OF CONSCIOUSNESS
IN THE HUMAN BODY

Dimensional analysis indicates that good candidate ranges for testing the electromagnetic-field component of consciousness can be found in the near-infrared spectrum. This region lies just below the threshold of the visible spectrum that is picked up by eye-cone structures.[41]

Human core body temperatures, ranging from 36.3°C to 37.5°C on a diurnal cycle, indicate that, applying Wien's law, a search should be conducted within the infrared spectrum in a bandwidth between 9.36425 microns and 9.32808 microns, near the center of the infrared portion of the radiant spectrum.[42]

Converting from wavelength, this range is equivalent to a frequency range of 30.3 gigahertz to 32.0 gigahertz, an enormously wide band compared to, for example, the FM radio frequency band, ranging from 87.0 to 108.1 MHz.[43] Assuming a bandwidth of 200 KHz (typically used for a single FM station), over 8,000 equivalent FM radio stations could be broadcast within the human infrared radiation band, with no overlapping interference.

One approach in the search for an infrared component of consciousness would be to monitor the dynamics of an infrared spectrum emanating from within the human body in an attempt to detect information-carrying photons escaping the body as modulated infrared radiation. It is possible to detect wavelengths down to 5 microns (the far-infrared region) using Fourier transform infrared spectroscopy and to record noninvasively site-specific emissions of infrared radiation issuing from within human organs.[44]

> Interestingly, because biologic materials are transparent to light in the near-infrared region of the light spectrum, transmission of photons through organs is possible.[45]

The next step would be to demodulate (decode) these photon-packet streams, the difficulty being that even in human communication technology there currently exist dozens of modulation techniques.[46]

An alternate approach would be to search for infrared energy signals flowing as patterns *within* potential physiological waveguide channels located within the human body. The ubiquitous blood capillary system, for example, with typical inner diameters of 10 microns, is a likely candidate to act as an infrared waveguide. Capillaries provide a ready-made

Eight Feasible Bands for Consciousness

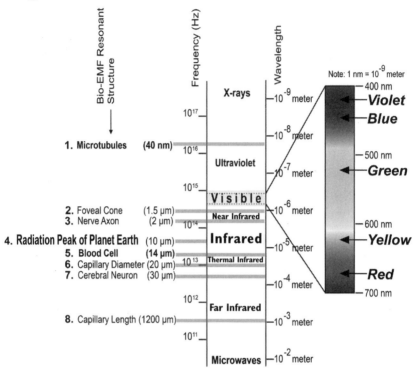

Fig. 8.6. Eight feasible electromagnetic radiation bands of consciousness. Possible bands of consciousness can be seen between ultraviolet and far infrared radiation. Adapted from Joye, "The Pribram-Bohm Holoflux Theory of Consciousness," 353.

network infrastructure within which the flow and resonance of a modulated infrared-energy plasma might be discovered. Figure 8.6 suggests the location of feasible electromagnetic bands of consciousness correlated with existing structural systems of the human body.

As indicated in figure 8.6, potential candidates for waveguide structures exist within the human body, ranging in diameter (recall that diameter correlates to a dipole wavelength resonant frequency) from ultraviolet radiation in microtubules at a wavelength of approximately 10^{-8} meter to far infrared radiation in erythrocytes in capillaries located in the 10^{-3} meter wavelength region.

But what does such technical information mean for those interested in experiencing new dimensions of awareness? First of all, it provides strong evidence that consciousness operates simultaneously within the body on multiple levels within distinctly separate channels or frequency ranges. It shows that consciousness is not constrained to a specific region of the brain behind the eyes within the cranial cavity. Indeed, when the brain shows no sign of activity (known clinically as "brain death"), are there not other systems of consciousness that must continue to run the many complex systems of the body that sustain life? The contemplative psychonaut should be aware that more than one system of consciousness is operational and that one can intentionally "tune in" to distinctly different regions and bandwidths of conscious activity within the body. Secondly, different systems of consciousness are operational in structural regions of different size ranges (such as the waveguides previously discussed at 10^{-3} meter and 10^{-8} meter). With practice, the psychonaut learns to "shrink down" awareness to increasingly small dimensions in order to tune in to ranges of supersensible information. The exact technique can only be mastered through experience, through intentional effort to sense the energies flowing at higher frequencies in the smaller dimensions within various regions and organs of the body. This approach has been elaborated by Steiner and has been developed and refined by Indian contemplatives for millennia. For example, we find a highly useful injunction given in the following passage from the *Vedānta Sutra,* a contemplative text that summarizes the basic teachings of the Vedāntic school of Indian philosophy. Composed sometime between 450 BCE and 200 CE, it stresses the importance of maintaining awareness in the heart region within an area "the size of the thumb" in order to commune with the true immortal Self.

> The person of the size of a thumb, the inner Self, is always settled in the heart of men. Let a man draw that Self forth from his body with steadiness, as one draws the pith from a reed. Let him know that Self as the Bright, as the Immortal.[47]

A similar practice of focusing intention within the heart region is known as the "Sacred Heart of Jesus" prayer, which began in the eleventh century among Benedictine monks. Over the centuries, praying while maintaining focus within the heart center has become widespread among many Christian contemplatives. We should also note here in passing the central role played by the human heart in diverse cultures, such as the important *Heart Sutra* in Buddhism, and the strong focus on the heart as an organ of transcendence in Aztec culture.

It is of primary importance for the contemplative to learn the technique of intentionally focusing consciousness for a sustained period (even if only for a minute or two) within a clearly selected internal region of human physiology such as the heart or the throat. Specific regions of the body have been identified in which enhanced cognitive powers can be evoked through contemplative concentration, and in the Indian subcontinent, as mentioned in Chapter 6, these regions have been termed chakras (wheels) by Patañjali and others. During the focus, special effort should be given to shrinking the region of attention down to smaller and smaller dimensions, guiding awareness as close to a point as possible, similar to the way one uses a magnifying glass to focus the rays of the sun on a point, leading to ignition. In the case of contemplative practice this "ignition" becomes a breakthrough into the supersensible.

CONCLUSION

We have examined plausible configurations of consciousness as radiant, information-encoded energy flowing and resonating not only throughout the cosmos but also within various regions of the human body. We close here with speculations for the future of human consciousness. It is reasonable to assume that, with the advent of new technologies, electronic devices will eventually harness these energies. Human consciousness will eventually be stored, duplicated, maintained, and manipulated through fiber optics, silicon, and perhaps metallic crystalline substrates rather than relying solely on biophysical animal tissue. It is increasingly conceivable that technologies will be developed for uploading consciousness from human beings into hardware with all of the advantages and unintended consequences that might ensue.

Yet such advances through the efforts of material science are likely not the only pathways for the expansion of consciousness in the near future. Mother nature has been steadily working for millennia to evolve new systems of awareness within the human body, and according to William A. Tiller, the eminent Stanford professor emeritus:

> My working hypothesis is that we are all spirits having a physical experience as we ride "the river of life" together. Our spiritual parents dressed us in our biobodysuits and put us in this playpen, which we call a universe, in order to grow in coherence, in order to develop our gifts of intentionality and in order to ultimately become what we were meant to become—effective cocreators.[48]

Volumes of esoteric work, both modern and ancient, urge us to begin a lifetime of exploration. Exhortations in these books assure us that the rewards will be as rich and of even greater significance than those offered by any experience in our day-to-day human lives. We are encouraged to develop ways of viewing reality that are only now beginning to awaken within our physical bodies. Using these enhanced abilities, we are told we will find the universe to be alive with consciousness, shimmering in vast networks of awareness far beyond anything we might have imagined. Psychonauts such as Rudolf Steiner, John Lilly, Teilhard de Chardin, the ancient sage Patañjali, and many others all relate similar accounts of their own visions within these wider realms. They encourage us to develop for ourselves the inner abilities to harness and direct the flow of consciousness within our bodies so that we too can lucidly navigate an ocean of reality beyond (and within) our familiar space-time cosmos. They assure us that we too can acquire the capabilities and skills to travel far within that transcendental, nondual ocean of the Self where others have traveled before, sailing into that mysterious region that Bohm termed the implicate order, and that others have referred to as the mind of God, the Void, and the Great Beyond.

The Mathematics of Consciousness

Mathematically, the space-time domain and the frequency domain are essential for human consciousness and for communication in all media. We find the first page of an electrical-engineering textbook highlighting the importance of Fourier mathematics in bridging the two domains.

> In describing signals, we use the two universal languages of electrical engineering—*time* and *frequency*. Strictly speaking, a signal is a function of time. However, the signal can be described equally well in terms of *spectral* or *frequency* information. As between any two languages, such as French and German, translation is needed to render information given in one language comprehensible in the other. Between time and frequency, the translation is effected by the *Fourier series* and the *Fourier integral*.[1]

Similarly, in his book *Brain and Perception,* the brain scientist Karl Pribram describes why organisms effectively use the same mathematics of the Fourier transform to bridge the frequency (spectral) domain and the space-time domain.

> It is reasonable to ask: What advantage does the organism gain by processing in the spectral transform domain? The answer is efficiency: The fact that correlations are *so easily achieved* by first convolving signals in the spectral domain and then, inverse trans-

forming them into the space-time domain. Thus Fast Fourier Transform (FFT) procedures have become the basis of computerized tomography, the CT scans used by hospitals.[2]

This emphasis on the significant role of Fourier transform mathematics in electrical engineering and neurophysiological research can also be found in quantum physics (e.g., on page 1 of Bohm's own 646-page textbook, *Quantum Theory*).

The development of the special mathematical techniques that are necessary for obtaining quantitative results in complex problems should take place, for the most part, either in a mathematics course or in a special course concerned with the mathematics of quantum theory. It seems impossible, however, to develop quantum concepts extensively without Fourier analysis. It is, therefore, presupposed that the reader is moderately familiar with Fourier analysis.[3]

This appendix provides a key to the basic mathematics underlying the Fourier transform by offering a history and step-by-step proof of the relationship of time to frequency, a concept that is important in electrical engineering, perception, and quantum physics.

LEONHARD EULER AND IMAGINARY NUMBERS

The two domains related by the Fourier transform, the time domain and frequency domain, had been "discovered," explored, and developed as early as 1735 by Leonhard Euler (1707–1783), a Swiss mathematical genius who not only defined the concept of a "function," (Euler was the first to write $f(x)$ to denote a function driven by a variable), but also named and defined numerous mathematical symbols widely used today, including the constant "pi," in Greek the letter π; he had determined through calculation that if the diameter of a circle is 1, its circumference on the other hand is an irrational number, 3.14159265 . . ., which "for the sake of brevity" he said he will call π.[4] Euler's most important published work is a two-volume textbook written in 1748, *Introductio ad analysin infinitorum* (*Introduction to Infinite Analysis*).[5]

> In the *Introductio*, Euler announced the dramatic discovery of a deep connection between exponential functions, trigonometric functions, and imaginary numbers. . . . Euler unveiled numerous discoveries about functions involving infinite theories . . . and proposed definitions and symbols that have since become standard, including π and e.[6]

An example can be seen here in his choice of a base for an exponential function, which he called e (for "Euler"), the sum of the following infinite series. The factional sign (!) is explained on page 146.

$$e = 1 + \frac{1}{1!} + \frac{1}{2!} + \frac{1}{3!} + \frac{1}{4!} + \frac{1}{5!} + \frac{1}{6!} + \frac{1}{7!} + \frac{1}{8!} + \frac{1}{9!} + \frac{1}{10!} + \frac{1}{11!} + \frac{1}{12!} + \cdots$$

This number e became Euler's base for what he called "natural logarithms," and one of the most important mathematical constants in modern physics.[7] However, Euler's greatest contribution to mathematical physics was his proof of an equation that established the link between the *time domain* and the *frequency domain*. The Nobel Prize–winning physicist Richard Feynman has called Euler's discovery "the gold standard for mathematical beauty" and "the most remarkable formula in mathematics."[8] The following pages explain this formula.

Mathematicians in the early eighteenth century, following Newton, sought expressions and patterns in pure mathematics that could be shown to mirror physical phenomena observed in nature. With his photographic memory and "rare ability for concentration," Euler was able to perceive patterns in mathematical series and relationships that resulted in a prodigious number of proofs. (At his death Euler had published more than forty folio volumes on mathematics.) Euler's biographer put forth his own theory on the spectacular success of this prodigy.

> The phenomenon "Euler" is essentially tied to three factors: first to the gift of a possibly unique memory. Anything Euler ever heard, saw,

or wrote, seems to have been firmly imprinted forever in his mind. For this, there are numerous contemporary testimonials. Still at an advanced age, he was known, for example, to delight members of his family, friends and social gatherings, with the literal (Latin) recitation of any song whatsoever from Vergil's *Aeneid* . . . not to speak of his memory for matters in mathematics. Secondly, his enormous mnemonic power was paired with a rare ability of concentration. Noise and hustle in his immediate vicinity barely disturbed him in his mental work: "A child on his knee, a cat on his back, this is the way he wrote his immortal works" reports his colleague Thiebault. The third factor of the "mystery Euler" is simply steady, quiet work.[9]

Prior to Euler's discovery, there had never been a way to mathematically connect the space-time (t_d) dimension with the nontemporal frequency (f_d) dimension. His discovery resulted from his investigation into an obscure field of mathematics (discovered by Greek mathematicians, but first called "imaginary numbers" by Descartes by way of ridicule) in which Euler defined the square root of minus one as the letter i (for "imaginary").* Thus the letter i designates the square root of minus one, and, conversely, $i^2 = -1$:

$$i = \sqrt{-1}$$

Euler found this imaginary number to be a great mathematical tool because multiplying i times i (i.e., squaring i), simply reverses the sign of an expression. This feature can be used to reverse the signs of various elements in a series expansion, and this allowed Euler to develop and explore a wide range of equalities in mathematical expansion series. Use of this imaginary number as an operator, combined with his copious memory, led directly to his discovery in 1735 of what is now called Euler's law: a direct relationship between real numbers and imaginary numbers. Depicted in

---

*While the i symbol continues to be used by mathematicians and physicists, electrical engineers use the letter j to designate imaginary numbers, primarily because they use the letter i to designate electrical current flow; see Kuo, *Network Analysis and Synthesis*, 16.

Cartesian coordinates, the horizontal axis of real numbers, commonly labeled the "time" axis, is widely used in physics and mathematical charting, while the vertical "imaginary" axis is widely used in electrical engineering because it governs so well the mathematics of complex-plane calculations that are ubiquitous in contemporary electronic devices, during the translation of digital to analog signals and vice versa.[10]

In his *Introductio ad analysin infinitorum,* Euler announced the discovery of a connection between exponential functions, trigonometric functions, and imaginary numbers.[11] Perhaps the best way to appreciate the beauty in the discovery of Euler's law is to go through its derivation.

DERIVATION OF EULER'S LAW

Euler was fascinated by what are called "infinite series," expressions by which trigonometric values can be expressed and, more importantly, calculated. By summing a series of arithmetical terms, the value of a sine or cosine of an angle can be calculated to any degree of precision by approximating them as the sum of a series of arithmetic values. Obviously, an entire infinite series could not be calculated, but approximations were acceptable because it allowed the creation of large tables of values that were in widespread demand for use by engineers throughout Europe in the sixteenth century.[12]

Euler spent countless hours developing various infinite series in the attempt to discover connections and relationships among the patterns. Two of these series especially intrigued him—the Scottish mathematician Colin Maclaurin's infinite series expansion of the sine and the cosine functions, both shown partially expanded as follows:

$$\sin x = x - \frac{x^3}{3!} + \frac{x^5}{5!} - \frac{x^7}{7!} + \frac{x^9}{9!} - \frac{x^{11}}{11!} \cdots$$

$$\cos x = 1 - \frac{x^2}{2!} + \frac{x^4}{4!} - \frac{x^6}{6!} + \frac{x^8}{8!} - \frac{x^{10}}{10!} \cdots$$

Note that the "factorial sign" (!) represents the product of all numbers starting from the indicated number down to 1, (i.e., $3! = 3 \times 2 \times 1 = 6$), and also that the ellipsis (...) in each of the expressions above indicates an infinite series of additional factors, which follow the same pattern of progression. When Euler discovered an infinite series expansion for his own natural logarithm (the base, used widely in nuclear physics, was later named *e* for Euler), he noticed how the Maclaurin series seemed similar to the pattern of expansion of his own discovery of the e^x expansion:

$$e^x = 1 + x + \frac{x^2}{2!} + \frac{x^3}{3!} + \frac{x^4}{4!} + \frac{x^5}{5!} + \frac{x^6}{6!} \cdots$$

Euler noticed that this was strangely similar to the Maclaurin expansions for *cos x* and *sin x* added together (shown below); the result of such an addition (the sum of the two series) is identical to the expansion of e^x, except where minus signs appear.

$$\sin x + \cos x = 1 + x - \frac{x^2}{2!} - \frac{x^3}{3!} + \frac{x^4}{4!} + \frac{x^5}{5!} - \frac{x^6}{6!} - \frac{x^7}{7!} + \frac{x^8}{8!} + \cdots$$

For many months Euler struggled to unlock the secret of what seemed to be a remarkably close connection. Finally, it dawned on him that the relationship might find closure if he could find a way to use his imaginary number *i*, the square root of minus 1, to change signs.

Substituting *ix* for *x* everywhere in his equation (an allowable substitution, since by the rules of algebra any valid expression can be substituted for *x*), he found that wherever i^2 could be identified and factored out, the sign for that expression would reverse, and he quickly saw that his expansion would then more closely match that of the expansion of *cos x + sin x*.

To recapitulate, here again is Euler's original infinite expansion of the natural logarithm that he had previously discovered:

$$e^x = 1 + x + \frac{x^2}{2!} + \frac{x^3}{3!} + \frac{x^4}{4!} + \frac{x^5}{5!} + \frac{x^6}{6!} \cdots$$

Wherever there is an *x* in the above equation, Euler substituted *ix*.

$$e^{ix} = 1 + ix + \frac{(ix)^2}{2!} + \frac{(ix)^3}{3!} + \frac{(ix)^4}{4!} + \frac{(ix)^5}{5!} + \frac{(ix)^6}{6!} \cdots$$

Wherever he found an i^2, Euler converted this to its value, -1.

$$e^{ix} = 1 + ix - \frac{x^2}{2!} - \frac{ix^3}{3!} + \frac{x^4}{4!} + \frac{ix^5}{5!} - \cdots$$

Rearranging the results slightly, we can see the original patterns of *cos x* and *sin x* expansion on the right, now seen as equal to Euler's e^{ix} (on the left); this equation is known as Euler's law.

$$e^{ix} = \left(1 - \frac{x^2}{2!} + \frac{x^4}{4!} - \cdots\right) + \left(ix - \frac{ix^3}{3!} + \frac{ix^5}{5!} - \cdots\right)$$

Now we factor out the i from the right side of the equation to get the following result:

$$e^{ix} = \left(1 - \frac{x^2}{2!} + \frac{x^4}{4!} - \cdots\right) + i * (x - \frac{x^3}{3!} + \frac{x^5}{5!} - \cdots)$$

The expressions now within the parentheses are simply the Maclaurin expansion series for *cos x* and *sin x,* and the entire expression can now be written as:

$$e^{ix} = \cos x + i * \sin x$$

The amazement generated by this discovery was that for the first time a solid, derivable mathematical link had been established between e, the natural exponential function, the imaginary number i, and trigonometric geometry.

$$\boldsymbol{e^{ix} = \cos x + i * \sin x}$$

Fig. A.1. Euler's Law.[13]

Notice how both sides of Euler's law contain both real numbers (x) and imaginary numbers (i). Euler's law maps the intersection of the axis of real numbers with the angular frequency axis of imaginary numbers on a single intersecting plane, allowing us to model mathematically the real world of space-time/frequency phenomena of quantum electrodynamics. Euler's law has since become the basis of electronic communication technology, within which our society is currently enmeshed.[14]

During the eighteenth century the field of "complex mathematics" remained an obscurity until "rediscovered" by physicists such as Maxwell, Tesla, and Marconi in the late nineteenth century; the mathematics of imaginary numbers became an essential tool for modeling an invisible electromagnetic reality and, more importantly, provided a direct way of calculating, predicting, and modulating the electromagnetic energy oscillations and waves associated with the newly emerging technologies of alternating current.[15] Nevertheless, it was Euler who first established the mathematical beachhead into the real-imaginary domain, and this relationship was eventually found, perhaps mysteriously, to mirror electromagnetic realities in space-time.[16]

INTEGRAL OPERATOR
AND FOURIER TRANSFORM

Seventy-four years after Euler published his famous theorem, Jean-Baptiste Joseph Fourier (1768–1830), expanding on Euler's mathematical discovery, published what came to be known as the Fourier series and the Fourier transform, in a book titled *The Analytic Theory of Heat.*[17] Before describing the Fourier transform, it is useful to begin by examining the word *integral* through the perspective of history. The word *integral* itself stems from a mathematical sign, a convention that was first introduced by Gottfried Wilhelm Leibniz (1646–1716) as a stylized, elongated letter *S* that he used as shorthand for the Latin word *summa* ("sum" or "total") to denote something that originates from a summation.[18]

Both Leibniz and Isaac Newton (1643–1727) seem to have developed the fundamental concepts of integral calculus simultaneously, but Newton's notation of using a vertical mark to indicate summation became the cause of considerable notational confusion (a vertical slash is "easily confused with the numeral 1, or with a bracket, or with the letter *I*), and over the next fifteen years Leibniz's elongated letter *S* found preference among mathematicians to denote "summation."[19]

The word *integral* itself was coined by Jacob Bernoulli (1654–1705), so that the *S* notation could more easily be discussed in mathematical conversation and in lectures.[20]

However, it was not until 1822, when Jean-Baptiste Joseph Fourier introduced the notation of upper and lower limits to the integral operator symbol, that the full power of integral calculus was unleashed, making possible the development of his "Fourier series."[21]

A full century after Euler, it was Fourier, working at the time as Napoleon's governor of Egypt, who managed to link the real and imaginary axes by building on Euler's theorem. While Euler had provided the initial link between the frequency and space-time domains, it was Fourier, during his experimental investigation of heat flow, who developed the mathematics to model the thermodynamic properties of energy and was able to derive a mathematical operation of integral calculus that accurately expressed the energy transformations between a time domain (t_d) and a frequency domain (f_d).[22]

It is our thesis here that the mathematics expressed in the Fourier transform can also be understood as a link between a physics of space-time (t_d) and an actual frequency domain (f_d).

The Fourier and inverse Fourier transforms are shown in the following equations:

$$f(t) = \int_{-\infty}^{+\infty} X(f)e^{j2\pi ft}\,df \qquad f(f) = \int_{-\infty}^{+\infty} x(t)e^{-j2\pi ft}\,dt$$

Fourier integral transform of a continuous frequency function into the *time domain* (t_d).   **Fourier integral transform of a continuous time function into the *frequency domain* (f_d).**

Fig. A.2. The Fourier transform and inverse transform.
See Stein and Shakarchi, Fourier Analysis, *134–36.*

These Fourier transform expressions indicate that any arbitrary function in the space-time domain, *f(t)*, can be transformed into and expressed by an infinite series of frequency spectra functions, *X(F)*, in the frequency domain and, conversely, that any arbitrary function in the frequency domain, *f(F)*, can be transformed into and expressed by an infinite series of time functions, *x(t)*.

These Fourier transforms are themselves derived from an underlying series of alternate pure sine and pure cosine waves, as depicted below in figure A.3.

$$f(t) = a_0 + \sum_{n=1}^{\infty} \left(a_n \cos \frac{n\pi t}{L} + b_n \sin \frac{n\pi t}{L} \right)$$

Fig. A.3. The Fourier series.
See Kuo, Network Analysis and Synthesis, 40.

THE FOURIER SERIES

A century after Fourier's death, Norbert Wiener made use of Fourier's transform to model and analyze brain waves, and he was able to detect frequencies, centered within different spatial locations on the cortex, that exhibited auto-correlation. Specific frequencies were found to be attracting one another toward an intermediate frequency, thus exhibiting resonance or "self-tuning" within a narrow range of the frequency domain (f_d).[23] This discovery led Wiener to conjecture that the infrared band of electromagnetic flux may be the loci of "self-organizing systems."[24]

> We thus see that a nonlinear interaction causing the attraction of frequency can generate a *self-organizing system*, as it does in the case of the brain waves we have discussed. . . . This possibility of self-organization is by no means limited to the very low frequency of these two phenomena. Consider self-organizing systems at the frequency level, say, of infrared light.[25]

Wiener goes on to discuss such possibilities in biology, where he focuses on the problems of communication at molecular and primitive cellular levels, specifically on the problem of how substances produce cancer by reproducing themselves to mimic preexisting normal local cells. Molecules do not simply pass notes to one another and they do not have eyes, so how do they perceive and how do they communicate? Wiener conjectures:

> The usual explanation given is that one molecule of these substances acts as a template according to which the constituent's smaller molecules lay themselves down and unite into a similar macromolecule. However, an entirely possible way of describing such forces is that the active bearer of the specificity of a molecule may lie *in the frequency pattern of its molecular radiation*, an important part of which may lie *in infrared electromagnetic frequencies* or even lower. It is quite possible that this phenomenon may be regarded as a sort of attractive interaction of frequency.[26]

At the end of his classic book on cybernetics, in the chapter, "Brain Waves and Self-Organizing Systems," Wiener suggests further possible studies to "throw light on the validity of my hypothesis concerning brain waves."[27] Wiener goes on to describe the widespread observations of seemingly simultaneous behavior of groups of living organisms such as crickets, tree frogs, or fish, activity that might be attributable to simultaneous synchronization of neuronal networks through resonant tuning within the frequency domain (f_d).

> It has often been supposed that the fireflies in a tree flash in unison. . . . I have heard it stated that in the case of some of the fireflies of Southeastern Asia this phenomenon is so marked that it can scarcely be put down to illusion. . . . Could not the same supposed phenomenon of the pulling together of frequencies take place? However this process occurs, it is a dynamic process and involves forces or their equivalent.[28]

REAL-IMAGINARY AND MANDELBROT'S SET

In early explorations of the real-imaginary domain model in the nineteenth century, the Danish mathematician Caspar Wessel (1745–1818), and the mathematical physicist and astronomer Johann Carl Friedrich Gauss (1777–1855) independently discovered that two-dimensional Cartesian plots or graphs could be made of the real-imaginary axes, with one axis of real numbers (traditionally illustrated by a straight horizontal line with values increasing from left to right) and a vertical axis of imaginary numbers drawn at a ninety-degree angle to the real number axis.[29] In the twentieth century this two-dimensional model had been adopted by electrical engineers to model, analyze, and solve complex problems dealing with transformations between the time (t_d) and frequency (f_d) domains in electrical power and communication engineering.[30] The concept remains at the essential core of engineering calculations for transforming electromagnetic energy into information encoded in light, sound, and multidimensional images.[31]

Perhaps the most fascinating tool for exploring the nature of the interface between the real and imaginary domains was developed in 1980 when the Polish American engineer Benoit Mandelbrot (1924–2010) created the software to plot an actual image of the two-dimensional interface between space-time and frequency domains close to the origin (defined as the intersecting point where the real axis equals zero and the imaginary axis equals zero). His initial impression, upon seeing the first image, was that the computer program had malfunctioned.[32] Subsequent computer plots assured him that these visual patterns were truly there. Images of this region about the time frequency origin have gained interest worldwide, and the region itself has come to be known as the Mandelbrot set, shown in figure A.4, on page 154. The English mathematical physicist Sir Roger Penrose was so taken by the resulting images that he described them with a sense of almost reverential awe.

> The Mandelbrot set is not an invention of the human mind: it was a discovery. Just like Mount Everest, the Mandelbrot set is just *there!*[33]

The Mandelbrot set exhibits remarkable properties. As calculations are done on ever smaller regions on the time-frequency plane, the images appear similar but never completely repeatable, and the viewer begins to

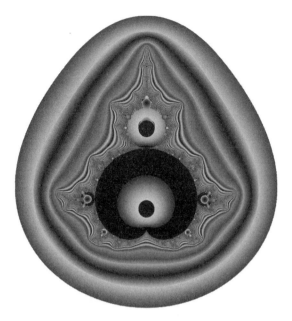

Fig. A.4. Mandelbrot: origin of real-imaginary axis.
An actual image of the two-dimensional interface between space-time
and frequency domains close to the origin (defined as the intersecting point
where the real axis equals zero and the imaginary axis equals zero).

sense some sort of biological shapes emerging from this strange world of pure mathematical being. Penrose goes on to say, "The very system of complex numbers has a profound and timeless reality which goes quite beyond the mental constructions of any particular mathematician."[34] The image also is reminiscent, perhaps, of a sitting Buddha!

Exploitation of the basic properties of this mysterious real-imaginary domain have led directly to twenty-first-century digital device systems, and accordingly, it is entirely conceivable that they might also be involved in some space-time-frequency spectrum of the psyche, as theorized by Jung: "Psychic processes therefore behave like a scale along which consciousness 'slides.'"[35]

Using the analogy of the spectrum, we could compare the lowering of unconscious contents to a displacement towards the red end of the colour band, a comparison which is especially edifying in that red, the blood colour, has always signified emotion and instinct. . . . The dynamism of instinct is lodged as it were in the nearer ranges of the infra-red part of the spectrum. . . . Psychologically, however, the archetype as a spiritual goal toward which the whole nature of man strives . . . as such is a psychoid factor that belongs, as it were, to the invisible, ultraviolet end of the psychic spectrum.[36]

Using Fourier analysis and the Fourier transform, signals can be described either as electromagnetic information in the time domain or holoflux information in the frequency domain, and this information is simultaneously transformed between the two domains. It can be said that they are two different aspects of one and the same thing, energy signals encoded with information content, but existing in both of two categorically distinct dimensions. In his groundbreaking essay, "On the Nature of the Psyche," Jung observes the relationship of psyche to matter with the same pattern, noting that they are two different modes of one and the same thing.

Since psyche and matter are contained in one and the same world, and moreover are in continuous contact with one another and ulti- mately rest on irrepresentable, transcendental factors, it is not only possible, but also fairly probable, even, that psyche and matter are two different aspects of one and the same thing.[37]

If we assume that the energy of the psyche expresses itself in the spectral frequency range within the human bio-system, as Jung has speculated, then a mathematical model of psychic energy activity might be found in the Fourier transform. Humans in contemporary society reliably experience the fruits of the mathematics of the Fourier transform every time a digital communication device is operated.[38]

For example, signal-processing chips in cell phones are encoded with what are called fast Fourier transform algorithms, which filter audio-voice-speech frequency patterns in the space-time domain into a relatively small set of pure frequencies, the individual amplitudes of which are then digitized and transmitted. On the receiving end, a reverse fast Fourier transform unpacks the frequency domain data, transforming them into space-time frequency waves of low voltage circuits, which then drive the vibrating speaker devices by which humans "hear" the re-created audio space-time spectral energy.[39]

Pribram describes this same process as it occurs in the brain, while emphasizing the difference between waves and spectra.

> Waves occur in space-time. Spectra do not. Spectra result from the interference among waves—and, by Fourier's insightful technique, the locus of interference can be specified as a number that indicates the "height" of the wave at that point. . . . Frequency in space-time has been converted to spectral density in the transform domain.[40]

The material in this Appendix has been presented in support of the underlying theme of this book, that there is a dimension of reality beyond space-time that can be entered into and perceived through a new mode of human awareness, a faculty that can be activated through sufficient knowledge and the requisite effort required to awaken this new mode of perception. The dimensions to be explored have been mapped by the mathematics of modern quantum theory, a theory that has become the cornerstone of our evolving global information network. This transcendent region (Bohm's implicate order) exists everywhere at the very center, congruent with and interpenetrating our space-time cosmos, inviting exploration by an alert human consciousness that is standing on the threshold of supersensible awareness.

Notes

INTRODUCTION

1. Crabtree, *From Mesmer to Freud.*

CHAPTER I.
FIVE APPROACHES TO
SUPERSENSIBLE PERCEPTION

1. Steiner, *Knowledge of the Higher Worlds,* 1.
2. Steiner, *Way of Self Knowledge,* 15.
3. Jibu and Yasue, *Quantum Brain Dynamics and Consciousness.*
4. Steiner, *Knowledge of the Higher Worlds,* 1.
5. Bryant, *Yoga Sutras of Patañjali,* 306.
6. Tookeram, *Yoga Aphorisms of Patañjali.*
7. Tookeram, *Yoga Aphorisms of Patañjali,* 140–41.
8. Furst, *Hallucinogens and Culture,* 108.
9. Fankhauser, *Hashish as a Drug,* 42.
10. Fankhauser, *Cannabis as Medicine,* 19.
11. Markel, *Anatomy of Addiction.*
12. Steiner, *Correspondence and Documents,* 16.
13. Steiner, *Correspondence and Documents,* 18.
14. Gonda, *History of Ancient Indian Religion,* 259.
15. Tookeram, *Yoga Aphorisms of Patañjali.*
16. Steiner, *Evolution of Consciousness,* 16.
17. Steiner, *Evolution of Consciousness,* 12.
18. Steiner, *Knowledge of the Higher Worlds,* 30.
19. Steiner, *Occult Physiology,* 95–96.
20. Steiner, *Knowledge of the Higher Worlds,* 27.

CHAPTER 2.
ACTIVATING AND CULTIVATING
SUPERSENSIBLE PERCEPTION

1. Steiner, *Evolution of Consciousness,* 16.

2. Steiner, *Evolution of Consciousness,* 16.

3. Steiner, *Evolution of Consciousness,* 16.

4. Steiner, *Evolution of Consciousness,* 20–21.

5. Steiner, *Evolution of Consciousness,* 33.

6. Steiner, *Evolution of Consciousness,* 33.

7. Flora, "God Almighty," 69.

8. Steiner, *Evolution of Consciousness,* 16.

9. Bryant, *Yoga Sutras of Patañjali,* 10; emphasis added.

10. Isaac the Syrian, *Ascetical Homilies.* Trans. from Greek and Syriac, 127.

11. Steiner, *Evolution of Consciousness,* 36.

12. Steiner, *Evolution of Consciousness,* 36.

13. Steiner, *Evolution of Consciousness,* 12.

14. Steiner, *Evolution of Consciousness,* 17.

15. Steiner, *Evolution of Consciousness,* 17.

16. Steiner, *Evolution of Consciousness,* 17.

17. Steiner, *Evolution of Consciousness,* 17.

18. Steiner, *Knowledge of the Higher Worlds,* 144.

CHAPTER 3.
THE FOUR DOMAINS OF THE HUMAN BEING

1. Steiner, *Evolution of Consciousness,* 33.

2. Steiner, *Occult Physiology,* 125.

3. Tiller, *Science of Crystallization.*

4. Powell, *Etheric Double,* 2–4.

5. Plato, "Vision of Er," *Republic,* 614.

6. Chlup, *Proclus: An Introduction,* 61.

7. Westenberg, *Max Heindel and the Rosicrucian Fellowship,* 17.

8. Wikipedia, "Astral Body"; see "Post-theosophists," par. 1.

9. Westenberg, *Max Heindel and the Rosicrucian Fellowship,* 34.

10. Steiner, *Occult Physiology,* 42.

11. Steiner, *Occult Physiology,* 44–45.

12. Jibu and Yasue, *Quantum Brain Dynamics and Consciousness.*

13. Fechner, *Religion of a Scientist,* 309.

14. Jibu and Yasue, *Quantum Brain Dynamics and Consciousness,* 164.

15. Jibu and Yasue, *Quantum Brain Dynamics and Consciousness,* 83.

16. Steiner, *Occult Physiology,* 44.

17. Steiner, *Occult Physiology,* 120.

18. McCraty, *Energetic Heart,* 17.

19. Steiner, *How to Know Higher Worlds,* 35.

20. Steiner, *Evolution of Consciousness,* 30.

CHAPTER 4.
CONDITIONS FOR SUPERSENSIBLE PERCEPTION

1. Steiner, *Knowledge of the Higher Worlds,* 111.

2. Steiner, *Knowledge of the Higher Worlds,* 112.

3. Steiner, *Knowledge of the Higher Worlds,* 113.

4. Steiner, *Knowledge of the Higher Worlds,* 108.

5. Steiner, *Knowledge of the Higher Worlds,* 108.

6. Steiner, *Knowledge of the Higher Worlds,* 108–9.

7. Steiner, *Evolution of Consciousness,* 36.

8. Isaac the Syrian, *Ascetical Homilies,* Homily #14, 201.

9. Lilly, *Programming and Metaprogramming in the Human Biocomputer.*

10. Steiner, *Knowledge of the Higher Worlds,* 146.

11. Michael, *Law of Attention,* 127.

CHAPTER 5.
MY JOURNEY FROM PHYSICS TO METAPHYSICS

1. Lilly, *Scientist,* 128.

2. Blofeld, *Wheel of Life.*

3. Churton. *Aleister Crowley: The Biography,* 108.

4. Blofeld, *Wheel of Life,* 149–50.

5. Blofeld, *Wheel of Life,* 150.

6. Ouspensky, *In Search of the Miraculous.*

7. Ouspensky, *In Search of the Miraculous,* 3.

8. Wood, *Practical Yoga: Ancient and Modern.*

9. Taimni, *Science of Yoga.*

10. Whicher, *Integrity of the Yoga Darśana,* 42.

11. Mishra, *Textbook of Yoga Psychology.*

CHAPTER 6.
INDIAN TANTRA AND SUPERSENSIBLE PERCEPTION

1. Gonda, *History of Ancient Indian Religion,* 4:251.

2. Taimni, *Gayatri,* 24.

3. Khanna, *Yantra,* 11.

4. Pandit, *Lights on the Tantra,* 15.

5. Rele, *Mysterious Kundalini,* 29.

6. Whicher, *Integrity of the Yoga Darśana,* 27.

7. Zambito, *Unadorned Thread of Yoga,* 10.

8. Bryant, *Yoga Sūtras of Patañjali,* xvii.

9. Author's translation of Sanskrit to English.

10. Author's translation of Sanskrit to English.

11. Eliade, *Yoga: Immortality and Freedom,* 326.

12. Bryant, *Yoga Sutras of Patañjali,* 306.

13. Whicher, *Integrity of the Yoga Darśana,* 2.

14. Rele, *Mysterious Kundalini.*

15. Rele, *Mysterious Kundalini,* 50.

16. Rele, *Mysterious Kundalini,* 54.

17. Rele, *Mysterious Kundalini,* 34.

CHAPTER 7.
THE COSMOLOGY OF CONSCIOUSNESS

1. Sullivan, "Interviews with Great Scientists," 17.

2. Sullivan, "Interviews with Great Scientists," 17.

3. Bohm, *Wholeness and the Implicate Order,* 193.

4. Carr, *Universe or Multiverse?* 10.

5. Carr, *Universe or Multiverse?* 13.

6. Wiener, *God and Golem, Inc.*

7. Joye, "The Pribram-Bohm Holoflux Theory of Consciousness," 261.

8. Bohm, *Wholeness and the Implicate Order*; Pribram, *Form Within.*

9. Bohm and Peat, *Science, Order, and Creativity,* 311–12.

10. Chalmers, *Character of Consciousness,* 5.

11. Bisson, "They're Made Out of Meat," 42.

12. Chalmers, *Character of Consciousness*, 25.

13. Chalmers, "Facing Up to the Problem of Consciousness," in *Character of Consciousness*, 26.

14. Chalmers, "Facing Up to the Problem of Consciousness," in *Character of Consciousness*, 27–28.

15. Chalmers, "Facing Up to the Problem of Consciousness," in *Character of Consciousness*, 27.

16. Wheeler, *Geons, Black Holes, and Quantum Foam*, 340.

17. Wheeler, *Geons, Black Holes, and Quantum Foam*, 340.

18. Wheeler, *A Journey into Gravity and Spacetime*, 154.

19. Pockett, *Nature of Consciousness*, 9–10.

20. Pockett, "Difficulties with the Electromagnetic Field Theory of Consciousness," 271.

21. Pockett, *Nature of Consciousness*, 88–89.

22. Pockett, *Nature of Consciousness*, 95.

23. McFadden, "Conscious Electromagnetic Information (CEMI) Field Theory."

24. McFadden, "Conscious Electromagnetic Field Theory," 262.

25. McFadden, "Synchronous Firing and Its Influence," 23.

26. Pribram, *Brain and Perception*, 238.

27. Edelman and Tononi, *Universe of Consciousness*, 215–19.

28. Skrbina, *Panpsychism in the West*, 1–2.

29. Bellah, *Religion in Human Evolution*.

30. Bohm, *Wholeness and the Implicate Order*; Pribram, *Form Within*.

31. Weber, "The Physicist and the Mystic," 187.

32. Bohm, *Wholeness and the Implicate Order*, 172.

33. Bohm, *Wholeness and the Implicate Order*, 159.

34. Feynman, Leighton, and Sands, *Feynman Lectures on Physics*, 286.

35. Kuo, *Network Analysis and Synthesis*, 13.

36. Wiener, *Cybernetics*, 11.

37. Wiener, *Cybernetics*, 181.

38. Wiener, *Cybernetics*, 191.

39. Wiener, *Cybernetics*, 198.

40. Wiener, *Cybernetics*, 202.

41. Bohm, *Quantum Theory*, 1.

42. James, *Varieties of Religious Experience*, 318.

43. Stein and Shakarchi, *Fourier Analysis: An Introduction,* 134–36.

44. Pribram, *Languages of the Brain.*

45. Pribram, "Prolegomenon for a Holonomic Brain Theory."

46. Pribram, *Form Within,* 82.

47. Pribram, *Languages of the Brain.*

48. Pribram, *Languages of the Brain,* xvii.

49. Pribram, *Languages of the Brain,* 142.

50. Pribram, "What the Fuss Is All About," 29.

51. Pribram, "Prolegomenon for a Holonomic Brain Theory."

52. Pribram, "Brain and Mathematics," 230.

53. Pribram, *Form Within.*

54. Pribram, "Consciousness Reassessed," 8.

55. Bohm and Hiley, *Undivided Universe,* 382.

56. Cazenave, *Science and Consciousness,* 1984.

57. Pribram, *Form Within.*

58. Pribram, *Form Within.*

59. Bohm and Hiley, *Undivided Universe,* 381–82. Emphasis added.

60. Bohm and Weber, "Nature as Creativity," 35–36.

61. Pribram, "Consciousness Reassessed," 13.

62. Pribram, *Brain and Perception,* 70.

63. Spencer-Brown, *Laws of Form,* 105.

64. Bohm, *Wholeness and the Implicate Order,* 190.

65. Bohm, *Wholeness and the Implicate Order,* 191.

66. Bohm, *Wholeness and the Implicate Order,* 151, 190, 172, and 192, respectively.

67. Bohm, *Wholeness and the Implicate Order,* 196 and 197.

68. Leibniz, *Monadology.*

69. Aristotle (trans. 2004) in Hakim, *Story of Science.*

70. Young, *Introduction to Hilbert Space.*

71. Bars and Terning, *Extra Dimensions in Space and Time,* 27.

CHAPTER 8.
THE PHYSIOLOGY OF CONSCIOUSNESS

1. Pribram, *Form Within;* Bohm, *Wholeness and the Implicate Order.*

2. Pribram *Form Within;* Bohm, *Wholeness and the Implicate Order.*

3. Chalmers, "Facing Up to the Problem of Consciousness"; Block, "On a

Confusion about a Function of Consciousness"; Bohm, *Wholeness and the Implicate Order*; Teilhard de Chardin, *Appearance of Man*; Laszlo, *The Self-Actualizing Cosmos*.

4. Dorf, *Electrical Engineering Handbook,* 1538.

5. Bohm, *Wholeness and the Implicate Order,* 77.

6. Bohm, *Wholeness and the Implicate Order,* 77.

7. Wheeler, *Journey into Gravity and Spacetime.*

8. Susskind, *Black Hole War.*

9. Wheeler, *A Journey into Gravity and Spacetime,* 222.

10. Bekenstein, "Black Holes and Entropy."

11. Romanes, *Cunningham's Textbook of Anatomy,* 137.

12. Hill, "Blueprints of NSA's Ridiculously Expensive Data Center," par. 7.

13. Joye, "Pribram-Bohm Holoflux Theory of Consciousness."

14. Bekenstein, "Black Holes and Entropy."

15. Bohm, *Wholeness and the Implicate Order,* 80.

16. Feynman, Leighton, and Sands, *Feynman Lectures on Physics,* 78.

17. Blakeslee, *Radio Amateur's Handbook,* 580.

18. Dorf, *Electrical Engineering Handbook.*

19. Dorf, *Electrical Engineering Handbook.*

20. Goward, "Visible-Near Infrared Spectral Reflectance," 194.

21. Chen, *Introduction to Plasma Physics,* 1.

22. Dorf, *Electrical Engineering Handbook,* 27.

23. McCraty, *Energetic Heart.*

24. Turgeon, *Clinical Hematology.*

25. Romanes, *Cunningham's Textbook of Anatomy.*

26. Wick, Pinggera, and Lehmann, *Clinical Aspects,* 6.

27. Fraser and Frey, "Electromagnetic Emission at Micron Wavelengths."

28. Teilhard de Chardin, "Phenomenon of Spirituality"; Steiner, *Occult Physiology.*

29. Teilhard de Chardin, "The Activation of Human Energy," 393.

30. Teilhard de Chardin, "The Atomism of Spirit," 29.

31. Teilhard de Chardin, "The Activation of Human Energy," 393.

32. Teilhard de Chardin, "The Activation of Human Energy," 378.

33. Steiner, *An Occult Physiology,* 42.

34. Steiner, *An Occult Physiology,* 43.

35. Pribram, *Languages of the Brain*; "Prolegomenon for Pribram, Holonomic Brain Theory."

36. Libet, *Mind Time,* 86–87.

37. Libet, *Mind Time.*

38. Bohm, *Unfolding Meaning,* 128.

39. Chalmers, *Character of Consciousness,* 5.

40. Dennett, *Consciousness Explained,* 406.

41. Oyster, *Human Eye.*

42. Becker, *Cross Currents: The Perils of Electropollution.*

43. Blakeslee, *Radio Amateur's Handbook.*

44. Griffiths and de Haseth, *Fourier Transform Infrared Spectrometry.*

45. Cohn, "Near-Infrared Spectroscopy," 323.

46. American Radio Relay League, *The ARRL 2016 Handbook,* 42.

47. Thibaut, *Vedanta-Sutras with the Commentary by Sankaracarya,* 198.

48. Tiller, *Psychoenergetic Science,* 47.

APPENDIX.
THE MATHEMATICS OF CONSCIOUSNESS

1. Kuo, *Network Analysis and Synthesis,* 1.

2. Pribram, *Brain and Perception,* 73.

3. Bohm, *Quantum Theory,* 1.

4. Crease, *Great Equations,* 100.

5. Crease, *Great Equations,* 98.

6. Crease, *Great Equations,* 98–99.

7. Crease, *Great Equations,* 100.

8. Feynman, Leighton, and Sands, *Feynman Lectures on Physics,* 211.

9. Fellmann, *Leonhard Euler,* xv.

10. Kuo, *Network Analysis and Synthesis,* 77.

11. Crease, *Great Equations,* 99.

12. Crease, *Great Equations,* 100.

13. Crease, *Great Equations,* 102.

14. Blakeslee, *Radio Amateur's Handbook,* 23.

15. Kuo, *Network Analysis and Synthesis,* 14.

16. Crease, *Great Equations,* 108.

17. Fourier, *Analytic Theory of Heat.*

18. Crease, *Great Equations,* 96.

19. Browder, *Mathematical Analysis: An Introduction,* 121.

20. Livio, *Golden Ratio: The Story of Phi.*

21. Feynman, Leighton, and Sands, *Feynman Lectures on Physics,* 271.

22. Feynman, Leighton, and Sands, *Feynman Lectures on Physics,* 286.

23. Wiener, *Cybernetics,* 198.

24. Wiener, *Cybernetics,* 198.

25. Wiener, *Cybernetics,* 202.

26. Wiener, *Cybernetics,* 202. Italics added.

27. Wiener, *Cybernetics,* 200.

28. Wiener, *Cybernetics,* 200.

29. Bell, *Men of Mathematics.*

30. Kuo, *Network Analysis and Synthesis.*

31. Kuo, *Network Analysis and Synthesis,* 389.

32. Mandelbrot, "Fractals and the Rebirth of Iteration Theory," 151.

33. Penrose, *Emperor's New Mind,* 124.

34. Penrose, *Emperor's New Mind,* 127.

35. Jung, "On the Nature of the Psyche," 207.

36. Jung, "On the Nature of the Psyche," 187–213.

37. Jung, "On the Nature of the Psyche," 215.

38. Brigham, "Fast Fourier Transform."

39. Brigham, "Fast Fourier Transform."

40. Pribram, *Form Within,* 109.

References

American Radio Relay League. *The ARRL 2016 Handbook for Radio Communications Software*. 93rd ed. Newington, Conn.: American Radio Relay League, 2015.

Bars, Itzhak, and John Terning. *Extra Dimensions in Space and Time*. New York: Springer, 2009.

Becker, Robert O. *Cross Currents: The Perils of Electropollution, the Promise of Electromedicine*. New York: Jeremy P. Tarcher/Penguin Books, 1990.

Bekenstein, Jacob D. "Black Holes and Entropy." *Physical Review* 7, no. 8 (1973): 2333–46.

Bell, E. T. *Men of Mathematics*. New York: Simon and Schuster, 1937.

Bellah, Robert. *Religion in Human Evolution: From the Paleolithic to the Axial Age*. Cambridge, Mass.: Harvard University Press, 2011.

Bisson, Terry. "They're Made Out of Meat." *Omni Magazine* 13. no. 7 (1990): 42–45.

Blakeslee, Douglas, ed. *The Radio Amateur's Handbook*. Newington, Conn.: American Radio Relay League, 1972.

Block, Ned. "On a Confusion about a Function of Consciousness." *Behavioral and Brain Science* 18, no. 2 (1995): 227–87.

Blofeld, John. *The Wheel of Life: The Autobiography of a Western Buddhist*. 2nd ed. Berkeley: Shambhala, 1972.

Bloom, Allan. *The Republic of Plato: Translated with Notes and an Interpretive Essay by Allan Bloom*. New York: Basic Books, 1968.

Bohm, David. *Quantum Theory*. New York: Prentice-Hall, 1951.

———. *Unfolding Meaning: A Weekend of Dialogue with David Bohm*. Edited by Donald Factor. Abingdon, UK: Routledge, 1985.

———. *Wholeness and the Implicate Order*. London: Routledge & Kegan Paul, 1980.

Bohm, David, and Basil J. Hiley. *The Undivided Universe: An Ontological Interpretation of Quantum Theory*. Abingdon, UK: Routledge, 1993.

Bohm, David, and F. David Peat. *Science, Order, and Creativity.* New York: Bantam Books, 1987.

Bohm, David, and R. Weber. "Nature as Creativity." *ReVision* 5, no. 2 (1982): 35–40.

Brigham, E. Oran. *The Fast Fourier Transform.* New York: Prentice-Hall, 2002.

Browder, Andrew. *Mathematical Analysis: An Introduction.* New York: Springer-Verlag, 1996.

Bryant, Edwin F. *The Yoga Sutras of Patañjali: A New Edition, Translation, and Commentary with Insights from Traditional Commentators.* New York: North Point Press, 2009.

Carr, Bernard, ed. *Universe or Multiverse?* Cambridge: Cambridge University Press, 2007.

Cazenave, Michael, ed. *Science and Consciousness: Two Views of the Universe; Edited Proceedings of the France-Culture and Radio-France Colloquium, Cordoba, Spain.* Translated by A. Hall and E. Callender. Oxford: Pergamon Press, 1984.

Chalmers, David J. *The Character of Consciousness.* New York: Oxford University Press, 2010.

———. "Facing Up to the Problem of Consciousness." *Journal of Consciousness Studies* 2, no. 3 (1995): 200–19.

Chen, Francis F. *Introduction to Plasma Physics and Controlled Fusion.* Vol. 1, *Plasma Physics.* 2nd ed. New York: Springer, 2006.

Chlup, Radek. *Proclus: An Introduction.* Cambridge: Cambridge University Press, 2012.

Churton, Tobias. *Aleister Crowley: The Biography.* Oxford: Watkins Publishing, 2011.

Cohn, Stephen M. "Near-Infrared Spectroscopy: Potential Clinical Benefits in Surgery." *Journal of the American College of Surgeons* 205, no. 2 (2007): 322–32.

Crabtree, Adam. *From Mesmer to Freud: Magnetic Sleep and the Roots of Psychological Healing.* New Haven, Conn.: Yale University Press, 1993.

Crease, Robert P. *The Great Equations: Breakthroughs in Science from Pythagoras to Heisenberg.* New York: W. W. Norton, 2008.

Dennett, Daniel. *Consciousness Explained.* New York: Back Bay Books, 1992.

Dewey, Barbara. *The Theory of Laminated Spacetime.* Inverness, Calif.: Bartholomew Books, 1985.

Dorf, Richard C., ed. *The Electrical Engineering Handbook.* 2nd ed. Boca Raton, Fla.: CRC Press, 1997.

Edelman, Gerald, and Giulio Tononi. *A Universe of Consciousness: How Matter Becomes Imagination.* New York: Basic Books, 2000.

Eliade, Mircea. *Yoga: Immortality and Freedom.* Princeton, N.J.: Princeton University Press, 2009.

Fankhauser, Manfred. *Cannabis as Medicine in Europe in the 19th Century.* Zurich: Swiss Society for the History of Pharmacy, 1992.

———. *Hashish as a Drug: The Importance of Cannabis Sativa in Western Medicine.* Zurich: Swiss Society for the History of Pharmacy, 2002.

Fechner, Gustav. *Elements of Psychophysics*, Translated by Helmut E. Adler. Boston: Holt, Rinehart, and Winston, 1966. First published 1860.

———. *Religion of a Scientist: Selections from Gustav Theodor Fechner.* New York: Pantheon, 1946.

Fellmann, E. A. *Leonhard Euler.* Translated by E. Gautschi. Basel, Switzerland: Birkhauser, 2007.

Feynman, Richard P., Robert Leighton, and Matthew Sands. *The Feynman Lectures on Physics.* Vol. 1. Reading, Mass.: Addison-Wesley, 1964.

Flora, Carlin. "God Almighty." *Psychology Today* 40, no. 3 (2007): 68–75.

Fourier, Jean-Baptiste Joseph. *The Analytic Theory of Heat.* Translated by Alexander Freeman. Cambridge: The University Press, 1878. Originally published as *Théorie Analytique de la Chaleur.* Paris: Firmin Didot Père et Fils, 1822.

Fraser, Allan, and Allan Frey. "Electromagnetic Emission at Micron Wavelengths from Active Nerves." *Biophysical Journal* 8, no. 6 (1968): 731–34.

Fraser, Craig G. *The Cosmos: A Historical Perspective.* Westport, Conn.: Greenwood Press, 2006.

Furst, Peter T. *Hallucinogens and Culture.* Novato, Calif.: Chandler & Sharp, 1976.

Gonda, Jan. *History of Ancient Indian Religion.* Vol. 4, *Selected Studies of Jan Gonda.* Leiden, Netherlands: E. J. Brill, 1975.

Goward, Samuel N., Karl M. Huemmrich, and Richard H. Waring. "Visible-Near Infrared Spectral Reflectance of Landscape Components in Western Oregon." *Remote Sensing of Environment* 47, no. 2 (February): 190–203.

Griffiths, Peter R., and James A. de Haseth. *Fourier Transform Infrared Spectrometry.* 2nd ed. Hoboken, N.J.: Wiley Interscience, 2007.

Hakim, Joy. *The Story of Science: Aristotle Leads the Way*. Washington, D.C.: Smithsonian Books, 2004.

Hawking, Stephen. *A Brief History of Time*. New York: Bantam Books, 1988.

Heindel, Max. *The Message of the Stars*. Oceanside, Calif.: The Rosicrucian Fellowship, 1973.

———. *The Rosicrucian Mysteries: An Elementary Exposition of Their Secret Teachings*. 6th ed. Laguna Beach, Calif.: The Rosicrucian Fellowship, 1975.

Hill, Karen. "Blueprints of NSA's Ridiculously Expensive Data Center in Utah Suggest It Holds Less Info Than Thought." *Forbes* online, July 24, 2013.

Isaac the Syrian, Saint. *The Ascetical Homilies of St. Isaac the Syrian*. Revised 2nd ed. Translated by the Holy Transfiguration Monastery. Boston: Holy Transfiguration Monastery, 2011.

James, William. *The Varieties of Religious Experience*. Helena, Mont.: Kessinger, 2004. First published 1902.

Jibu, Mari, and Kunio Yasue. *Quantum Brain Dynamics and Consciousness: An Introduction*. Philadelphia: John Benjamins, 1995.

———. "Quantum Brain Dynamics and Quantum Field Theory." In *Brain and Being: At the Boundary between Science, Philosophy, Language, and Arts*, edited by Gordon Globus, Karl H. Pribram, and Giuseppe Vitiello, 267–90. Philadelphia: John Benjamins, 2004.

Joye, Shelli Renée. *The Little Book of Consciousness: Holonomic Brain Theory and the Implicate Order*. Viola, Calif.: The Viola Institute, 2017.

———. *The Little Book of the Holy Trinity: A New Approach to Christianity, Indian Philosophy, and Quantum Physics*. Viola, Calif.: The Viola Institute, 2017.

———. "The Pribram-Bohm Holoflux Theory of Consciousness: An Integral Interpretation of the Theories of Karl Pribram, David Bohm, and Pierre Teilhard de Chardin." Ph.D. diss., California Institute of Integral Studies, 2016.

———. *Tuning the Mind: Geometries of Consciousness*. Viola, Calif.: The Viola Institute, 2017.

Judge, William. *The Yoga Aphorisms of Patañjali*. Los Angeles: The Theosophical Company, 1889.

Jung, C. G. "On the Nature of the Psyche." Originally published in 1946, included in Vol. 8 of *The Collected Works of C. G. Jung*, 2nd ed. Translated by R. F. C. Hull. Princeton, N.J.: Princeton University Press, 1964.

Khanna, Madhu. *Yantra: The Tantric Symbol of Cosmic Unity*. London: Thames & Hudson, 1979.

Kuo, Franklin. *Network Analysis and Synthesis*. New York: Wiley, 1962.

Lachman, Gary. *Rudolf Steiner: An Introduction to His Life and Work*. London: Jeremy Tarcher, 2007.

Laszlo, Ervin. *The Self-Actualizing Cosmos: The Akasha Revolution in Science and Human Consciousness*. Rochester, Vt.: Inner Traditions, 2014.

Leibniz, Gottfried Wilhelm. *The Monadology*. Abingdon, UK: Routledge, 2015.

Leonard, George. *Mastery: The Keys to Success and Long-Term Fulfillment*. New York: Plume, 1992.

Libet, Benjamin. *Mind Time: The Temporal Factor in Consciousness*. Cambridge, Mass.: Harvard University Press, 2004.

Lilly, John. *Programming and Metaprogramming in the Human Biocomputer: Theory and Experiments*. New York: Communication Research Institute, 1968.

———. *The Scientist: A Metaphysical Autobiography*. Berkeley: Ronin Publishing, 1997.

Livio, Mario. *The Golden Ratio: The Story of Phi, the World's Most Astonishing Number*. New York: Broadway Books, 2003.

Mandelbrot, Benoit. "Fractals and the Rebirth of Iteration Theory." In *The Beauty of Fractals: Images of Complex Dynamical Systems*, by H.-O. Peitgen and P. H. Richter, 151–60. Berlin: Springer-Verlag, 1986.

Markel, Howard. *An Anatomy of Addiction: Sigmund Freud, William Halstead, and the Miracle Drug, Cocaine*. New York: Random House, 2011.

McCraty, Rollin. *The Energetic Heart: Bioelectromagnetic Interactions within and between People*. Boulder Creek, Calif.: Institute of HeartMath, 2003.

McFadden, Johnjoe. "Conscious Electromagnetic Field Theory." *NeuroQuantology* 5, no. 3 (2007): 262–70.

———. "The Conscious Electromagnetic Information (CEMI) Field Theory: The Hard Problem Made Easy." *Journal of Consciousness Studies* 9, no. 8 (2002): 45–60.

———. "Synchronous Firing and Its Influence on the Brain's Electromagnetic Field: Evidence for an Electromagnetic Field Theory of Consciousness." *Journal of Consciousness Studies* 9, no. 4 (2002): 23–50.

Michael, Edward Salim. *The Law of Attention: Nada Yoga and the Way of Inner Vigilance*. Rochester, Vt.: Inner Traditions, 2010.

Mishra, Rammurti S. *The Textbook of Yoga Psychology*. New York: The Julian Press, 1971.

National Institute of Standards and Technology website. "Fundamental Physical Constants: Planck Time." Accessed April 17, 2018.

Ouspensky, Piotr Demianovich (P. D.). *In Search of the Miraculous: Fragments of an Unknown Teaching*. New York: Harcourt, 1949.

Oyster, Clyde W. *The Human Eye: Structure and Function*. Sunderland, Mass.: Sinauer Associates, 1999.

Pandit, M. P. *Lights on the Tantra*. Madras, India: Ganesh & Co, 1957.

Peat, F. David. *Infinite Potential: The Life and Times of David Bohm*. Reading, Mass.: Addison-Wesley, 1997.

Penrose, Sir Roger. *The Emperor's New Mind: Concerning Computers, Minds, and the Laws of Physics*. New York: Oxford University Press, 1989.

Plato. *The Republic*. Translated by Benjamin Jowett. London: Clydesdale Press, 2018. First published 1871.

Pockett, Susan. "Difficulties with the Electromagnetic Field Theory of Consciousness: An Update." *NeuroQuantology* 5, no. 3 (2007): 271–75.

———. *The Nature of Consciousness: A Hypothesis*. Lincoln, Neb.: Writers Club Press, 2000.

Powell, Arthur E. *The Etheric Double*. Madras, India: The Theosophical Publishing House, 1925.

Pribram, Karl. "Brain and Mathematics." In *Brain and Being: At the Boundary between Science, Philosophy, Language, and Arts*, edited by Gordon Globus, Karl H. Pribram, and Giuseppe Vitiello, 215–40. Philadelphia: John Benjamins, 2004.

———. *Brain and Perception: Holonomy and Structure in Figural Processing*. Hillsdale, N.J.: Lawrence Erlbaum Associates, 1991.

———. "Consciousness Reassessed." *Mind and Matter* 2, no. 1 (2004): 7–35.

———. *The Form Within: My Point of View*. Westport, Conn.: Prospecta Press, 2013.

———. *Languages of the Brain: Experimental Paradoxes and Principles in Neuropsychology*. Englewood Cliffs, N.J.: Prentice-Hall, 1971.

———. "Prolegomenon for a Holonomic Brain Theory." In *Synergetics of Cognition: Proceedings of the International Symposium at Schloss Elmau, Bavaria, June 4–8, 1989*, edited by Hermann Haken and Michael Stadler, 150–84. Berlin, Germany: Springer-Verlag, 1990.

———. "What the Fuss Is All About." In *The Holographic Paradigm and Other Paradoxes*, edited by Ken Wilber, 27–34. Boulder, Colo.: Shambhala, 1982.

Rele, Vasant. *The Mysterious Kundalini: The Physical Basis of the "Kundalini Yoga."* Bombay, India: D. B. Taraporevala Sons, 1927.

Romanes, G., ed. *Cunningham's Textbook of Anatomy.* 10th ed. New York: Oxford University Press, 1964.

Sculley, Robert J., and Marlan O. Sculley. *The Demon and the Quantum: From the Pythagorean Mystics to Maxwell's Demon and Quantum Mystery.* Weinheim, Germany: Wiley-VCH, 2007.

Shannon, C. E. "A Mathematical Theory of Communication." *Bell System Technical Journal* 27 (1948): 623–56.

Sheldrake, Rupert. *A New Science of Life: The Hypothesis of Morphic Resonance.* Rochester, Vt.: Park Street Press, 1981.

Skrbina, David F. *Panpsychism in the West.* Cambridge, Mass.: MIT Press, 2017.

Smolin, Lee. "Atoms of Space and Time." In *A Question of Time: The Ultimate Paradox*, edited by Scientific American. Kindle DX version. New York: Scientific American, 2012 (title no longer available).

Spencer-Brown, George. *Laws of Form.* New York: Julian Press, 1972.

Stein, Elias M., and Rami Shakarchi. *Fourier Analysis: An Introduction.* Princeton, N.J.: Princeton University Press, 2003.

Steiner, Rudolf. *Correspondence and Documents, 1901–1925.* South Hampton, England: Camelot Press, 1988.

———. *The Evolution of Consciousness as Revealed through Initiation-Knowledge: Thirteen Lectures Given at Penmaenmawr, North Wales, 19th to 31st August, 1923.* 2nd ed. Translated by V. E. W. and C. D. Sussex, UK: Rudolph Steiner Press, 1966.

———. *How to Know Higher Worlds: A Modern Path of Initiation.* Translated by Christopher Bamford. Hudson, N.Y.: Anthroposophic Press, 1994.

———. *Knowledge of the Higher Worlds and Its Attainment.* 3rd ed. Translated by George Metaxa. New York: Anthroposophic Press, 1947.

———. *An Occult Physiology: Eight Lectures by Rudolf Steiner, Given in Prague, 20th to 28th March, 1911.* 2nd ed. London: Rudolf Steiner Publishing, 1951.

———. *A Way of Self Knowledge and the Threshold of the Spiritual World.* London: Steiner Books, 2006. First published 1975.

Sullivan, J. W. N. "Interviews with Great Scientists VI. Max Planck." *The Observer,* January 25, 1931.

Susskind, Leonard. *The Black Hole War: My Battle with Stephen Hawking to Make the World Safe for Quantum Mechanics.* New York: Little, Brown and Company, 2008.

Taimni, Iqbal Kishen (I. K.). *Gayatri: The Daily Religious Practice of the Hindus.* Wheaton, Ill.: Quest Books, 1989.

———. *The Science of Yoga: The Yoga-Sutras of Patañjali in Sanskrit with Transliteration in English and Commentary.* Madras, India: The Theosophical Publishing House, 1951.

Teilhard de Chardin, Pierre. "The Activation of Human Energy," In *Activation of Energy*, translated by R. Hague, 359–93. London: William Collins Sons, 1953.

———. *The Appearance of Man.* Translated by J. M. Cohen. New York: Harper & Row, 1956.

———. "The Atomism of Spirit," In *Activation of Energy*, translated by R. Hague, 21–57. London: William Collins Sons, 1953.

———. "The Phenomenon of Spirituality," In *Human Energy*, translated by J. M. Cohen, 93–112. New York: Harcourt Brace Jovanovitch, 1969. First published 1937.

"Theodore Pelecanos." Wikipedia. Last modified October 14, 2017.

Thibaut, George, trans. *The Vedanta-Sutras with the Commentary by Sankaracarya. Part I.* Oxford, Clarendon Press, 1890.

Tiller, William A. *Psychoenergetic Science: A Second Copernican-Scale Revolution.* Walnut Creek, Calif.: Pavior, 2007.

———. *Science and Human Transformation: Subtle Energies, Intentionality, and Consciousness.* Walnut Creek, Calif.: Pavior, 1997.

———. *The Science of Crystallization: Macroscopic Phenomena and Defect Generation.* Cambridge: Cambridge University Press, 1992.

Tookeram, Tatya. *The Yoga Aphorisms of Patañjali.* Bombay, India: Theosophy Company, 1885.

Turgeon, Mary Louise. *Clinical Hematology: Theory and Procedures.* 5th ed. Baltimore, Md.: Lippincott Williams & Wilkins, 2012.

Washburn, Michael. *Embodied Spirituality in a Sacred World.* Albany: State University of New York Press, 2003.

Waters-Bennett, Josephine. "Milton's Use of the Vision of Er." *Modern Philology* 36, no. 4 (1939): 351–58.

Weber, Renée. "The Physicist and the Mystic—Is a Dialogue Between Them Possible?" In *The Holographic Paradigm and Other Paradoxes: Exploring the Leading Edge of Science*, edited by Ken Wilber, 187–214. Boulder, Colo.: Shambhala, 1982.

Westenberg, Ger. *Max Heindel and the Rosicrucian Fellowship.* The Hague: Stichting Zeven, 2009.

Wheeler, John Archibald. *Geons, Black Holes, and Quantum Foam: A Life in Physics*. New York: W. W. Norton, 1998.

———. *A Journey into Gravity and Spacetime*. New York: Scientific American, 1990.

Whicher, Ian. *The Integrity of the Yoga Darśana: A Reconsideration of Classical Yoga*. Albany: State University of New York Press, 1998.

Whitehead, Alfred North. *Process and Reality: An Essay in Cosmology. Gifford Lectures, 1927–28*. New York: Simon & Schuster, 1978. Originally published in New York under the same title by Macmillan, 1929.

Wick, Manfred, Germar-Michael Pinggera, and Paul Lehmann. *Clinical Aspects and Laboratory. Iron Metabolism and Anemias*. 6th ed. New York: Springer-Verlag, 2011.

Wiener, Norbert. *Cybernetics: or Control and Communication in the Animal and the Machine*. Cambridge, Mass.: MIT Press, 1948.

———. *God and Golem, Inc.: A Comment on Certain Points Where Cybernetics Impinges on Religion*. Cambridge, Mass.: MIT Press, 1964.

Wood, Ernest E. *Practical Yoga: Ancient and Modern*. New York: E. P. Dutton & Co., 1948.

Young, Nicholas. *An Introduction to Hilbert Space*. Cambridge: Cambridge University Press, 1988.

Zambito, Salvatore. *The Unadorned Thread of Yoga: The Yoga-Sutra of Patañjali in English—A Compilation of English Translations*. Poulsbo, Wash.: Yoga-Sutras Institute Press, 1992.

Index